THE ART OF PAUSING

To Toto,

With appreciation
for your great spirit,
Keep painting, Keep
writing, Keep pausing.
Blessings,
Judy J.

THE ART OF PAUSING

Meditations for
the Overworked and Overwhelmed

Edited by Judith Valente

Poems and Reflections by
Judith Valente – Brother Paul Quenon, OCSO – Michael Bever

Photographs by
Brother Paul Quenon, OCSO

acta
PUBLICATIONS

THE ART OF PAUSING
Meditations for the Overworked and Overwhelmed

Edited by Judith Valente
Poems and Reflections by Judith Valente, Brother Paul Quenon, OCSO,
& Michael Bever and Photographs by Brother Paul Quenon, OCSO

Cover and text design by Patricia A. Lynch
Cover photo by Brother Paul Quenon, OCSO

Copyright © 2013 by Judith Valente, Paul Quenon, and Michael Bever

Published by ACTA Publications, 4848 N. Clark Street, Chicago, IL 60640,
(800) 397-2282, www.actapublications.com

Library of Congress Number: 2013941919
ISBN: 978-0-87946-509-4
Printed in the United States of America by United Graphics
Year 25 24 23 22 21 20 19 18 17 16 15 14
Printing 20 19 18 17 16 15 14 13 12 11 10 9 8 7 6 5 4 3 2

TABLE OF CONTENTS

PAUSES WRITTEN ON OUR DAYS

Perhaps you are sipping a steaming cup of tea at the breakfast table. Out of the corner of your eye, you catch a robin swoop down and settle on a window sill. You stop. You watch the bird through the glass and it watches you. You note the amber barrel of its chest, the flint-like eyes. The encounter lasts but seconds. Then you both fly away.

Or perhaps you are standing at a busy intersection during rush hour in a large city. Suddenly a pink message slip floats to the pavement, carried on the wind. It has drifted out of an office window or slipped from a pedestrian's shoulder bag. You imagine the journey that this slip of paper has traveled, the person for whom it was meant, who now might never receive its message.

Or perhaps you are chanting the Psalms at dawn in the towering chapel of a secluded monastery. As the singing pauses, you hear a monk's hungry stomach growl. The sound offers an odd counterpoint to the chant's melodic line and reminds you of your abject humanness even in the midst of grandeur.

All three incidents reflect moments in stasis. They seem to interrupt the flow of time. We stop, look, listen. These are haiku moments.

Throughout the ages, Japanese poets have written brief meditations aimed at drawing out something of the sacred in every season. For the contemporary person seeking to slow down amid the tyranny of Twitter, the stress of the slow commute, and the seemingly endless demands of work and family, haiku moments provide pauses written on our days. Those who honor these moments share something in common with the African tribesmen who stop periodically while traveling on safari. The tribesmen pause to allow their souls to catch up with them on the journey. It is both a time of rest and a time of awakening. Sooner or later, we all need to let our souls catch up with the rest of our lives.

This book of such moments, accompanied by brief verbal or photographic reflections, is an attempt to do just that. It is meant especially for those who, like me, want to live a more contemplative life but rarely have the luxury of pausing throughout the day to pray the Psalms, or sit quietly with a candle burning, meditating for a half hour in the same chair every day. It is for those of us who are overworked and yearn for moments of respite in between rushing to catch a plane, respond to email, do the laundry, change a diaper, or meet the other myriad demands of our 24/7 world.

The Benedictine writer Imogene Baker once described the contemplative life simply as "be where you are and do what you're doing." Like the way of contemplation, poetry propels us toward a state of heightened attentiveness. Of all the poetic forms, haiku might well be the most contemplative. These slender threads of writing lead us toward T.S. Eliot's "still point" of the mind where we encounter the marrow of an experience, what Eliot called "the dance."

The poems and reflections set down here are the work of three writers who inhabit very different worlds. But for each of us, the reading and writing of haiku is an essential spiritual practice. Brother Paul Quenon is a Trappist monk of the Abbey of Gethsemani who studied under the great spiritual writer, Thomas Merton. Brother Paul writes from the confines of a cloister and with the boundlessness of one who has spent a lifetime contemplating what really matters. He is the author of four books of poetry and a talented photographer. His images accompany many of the poems and reflections in this book. Michael Bever is a retired educator, a doctor of theology and an ordained Disciples of Christ minister who was drawn later in life to Catholic traditions. He combines Zen and Sufi practices with his Christian heritage. I am a broadcast journalist who covers religion news for PBS-TV and the author of two poetry collections and a book on contemporary monastic life. As a retreat leader, I try to help busy professionals like myself slow down, find more balance and tap into the transcendence of the everyday.

Brother Paul, Michael and I may write from different vantage points, but we are fellow travelers on the same journey. Our quest is to uncover something of the particular and, perhaps, the peculiar. In that sense, we share much in common with the tea master Sen yo Rikyu who recognized the preciousness of "one time, one meeting." With our haiku practice, the three of us seek to memorialize something of each day.

For Brother Paul, the writing of haiku is an integral part of his daily meditation practice. "In meditation, I aim for a simple awareness of the present moment," he once told me. "My haiku is an articulation of the gift of that moment, a brief conclusion to the time spent in silence. Being short, the haiku will not become just another distraction." For me, the reading and writing of haiku insures that I experience at least a few brief moments of stillness and silence daily. It leaves me with a greater sense of having *lived* the day. Michael came to haiku after suffering a stroke and enduring years of heart disease. The meditative practice of writing not only sustains his soul, but also strengthens, in every sense of the word, his heart.

This book, like the best haiku, grew out of happenstance, serendipity and the urge to connect with others. I first met Brother Paul in October 2008 when I was sent by the national PBS-TV program *Religion & Ethics Newsweekly* to report on the fortieth anniversary of Thomas Merton's death. Merton had been Brother Paul's novice director and had encouraged him to write poetry. When Brother Paul told me he wrote a haiku a day, often after long meditative walks, I became intrigued.

I boldly suggested that we begin a haiku exchange. I thought it would be interesting to see what emerged from our diverse environments. He writes as one steeped in silence and the ancient prayer rituals of monastic life. His surroundings are 4,000 acres of woods, lakes and fields in central Kentucky. I write as a modern, married professional woman living in both the metropolis of Chicago and the college town of Normal (significance noted!) in central Illinois.

At first we were like two people in the early stages of dating — each a bit unsure of how to relate to the other. Brother Paul's haiku were honed by years of practice and patient observation. Mine were often dashed off on scraps of paper in short pauses during my work day or when riding in a train or a taxi. His resembled delicate water color paintings. Mine often fell back on my journalistic training, presenting black and white images of the events of my day. Some even referenced the news. Eventually, I learned from Brother Paul to not merely record the story of my day but to look beyond to the story *behind* the story.

After two years of riding in this virtual van together, Brother Paul and I added Michael as a welcomed hitchhiker. Michael lives in Claremont, California, at the base of the San Gabriel Mountains, a far different landscape from the rolling knobs of Brother Paul's Kentucky or my central Illinois prairie.

For Michael, haiku is a lightning flash that illuminates a particular moment for both writer and reader. He seeks in that moment what a photographer might call the puntus in a photographic image — the center of attention. He taught me that it is not necessary to explain a haiku, or even to understand it. What is essential is to ponder.

In this book, we have followed the classic form of English-language haiku: three lines of five, seven and five syllables. Over the centuries, haiku masters have experimented widely. Some haiku contain more than 17 syllables, others consist of merely one line, like this one by the American poet Allen Ginsberg, written not long before his death:

To see Void, vast infinite, look out the window into blue sky.

Another haiku writer compressed a surfeit of experience into a single word: *tundra*.

Most classic haiku describe a scene in nature and many reference a particular season. Here, you will find many haiku that arise out of urban and suburban as well as rural settings. "I take my poems where I find them," said the great modernist poet William Carlos Williams, a pediatrician by profession. Whatever the setting, whatever the word count or number of lines, all haiku share a common impetus: the distillation of experience.

Whenever I have the chance, I encourage people to write a haiku each day. It is a practice that monastic scholar Jonathan Montaldo calls "writing a holy sentence everyday." I suggest they find a partner or partners with whom they can exchange their haiku. People often end up pairing with someone they've known for years, in their community or their church, but had never *really* known. The haiku exchange is a way of building community and recognizing that none of us, alone, has a lock on truth or insight.

Our hope is that you will use this book as a springboard for your personal pausing or for initiating a haiku exchange. The poems — along with our reflections and the photographs by Brother Paul that accompany them — will help you to uncover your own haiku moments. We hope they inspire you to "write a holy sentence everyday" in silence, for silence is the door to contemplation.

Each haiku presented here seeks to illuminate one of the 99 names of God referred to in sacred texts. For God, the Restorer; God, the Compeller; God, the Compassionate; God, the Designer: God, the Determiner; God, the Subtle and Profound, is present in the world in these and other manifestations everywhere and every day. According to tradition, the 100th name of God cannot be known or spoken. Like some of the greatest haiku, it is pure mystery.

Of utmost importance, though, is that you simply enjoy yourself as you pause. If you sometimes feel overwhelmed by your life, we invite you to be like the wise chair in this haiku by Michael:

Two blue chairs sitting
One contemplates brass Buddha
Other simply sits

Judith Valente
Normal, Illinois

POEMS, PHOTOGRAPHS, REFLECTIONS

ON THE NAMES OF GOD

GOD, THE FIRST

Ninety-nine bows to
ninety-nine glimpses of God
eluding vision

                                              P Q

GOD, THE GUIDE

Calendar dates X'd
Leaves removed from old year's tree
Their stories written

JV

When I was younger, my life seemed to spread before me, an endless highway. But somewhere in my thirties, the road began to feel more like the Indianapolis Speedway. First months, then years, flashed by at race-car speed. I felt as though I barely had begun to process the events of one year before a new year sprang upon me.

One New Year's Eve, instead of partying with friends, I went on a spiritual retreat. The retreat leader suggested we look back month by month at the year just passed and jot down a few memories from each month. Ever since then, I've made this little exercise an annual practice. Under closer scrutiny, years in which I thought I'd wasted so much time suddenly seemed chock full of my half-forgotten accomplishments. Occasionally, I've been able to connect the threads between years in such a way as to see a clear pattern leading me in a new direction.

Each January around the time of the first new moon, I write a letter to myself detailing my hopes for the coming year. The letter is more than a to-do list or an enumeration of goals. It is like writing the prologue of the year ahead, fleshing out its plot. I seal the letter in an envelope and then don't read it again until the following January. Opening that envelope, I'm often gripped by a sense of dread. Will I have accomplished what I set out to do or experienced what I had hoped for? Sometimes I put off reading the letter clear into spring! Inevitably, I'm surprised each time by just how much the past year did fulfill my expectations and then some. My anxiety, as usual, was unnecessary. It may feel at times as though I am sleep-walking through my days. But life is always progressing. Goethe once wrote of a drunken beggar on horseback. What mattered, he said, was not that the beggar was drunk and reeling, but that he was mounted on his horse and, however imperfectly, was going somewhere.

GOD, THE LIGHT

Crowded train station
Bow to deep lotus presence
in each sad rider

JV

One of the reasons I enjoy train travel so much is that these journeys often afford unexpected glimpses into everyday life. Once, a train I was riding stopped at night in a small town. In a lighted kitchen, I spotted a young mother toweling dry her young son fresh from his bath. Sometimes the train will pause long enough beside someone's backyard for me to read the hieroglyphs of a clothes line: a woman's night gown, a man's stenciled work shirt, a girl's school uniform. Each offers a clue to the family's life within. At still another stop, I spotted a man in a red shirt stretched out beneath an underpass, smoking a cigarette. What was he doing there? What in the world was he thinking? I later even questioned whether I had actually seen the man. Perhaps the little boy just out of the bath, the person who hung out the laundry or the lone man smoking a cigarette caught sight of my face in the train window and wondered about me too.

In his book, *Man's Search for Meaning*, the psychiatrist Viktor E. Frankl writes of experiencing unimaginable cruelties in a Nazi prison camp. One morning, nearly delirious from hunger, Frankl was ordered to dig a trench in the numbing cold. He struggled to find any shred of meaning for his relentless suffering, his slow dying. At that moment, a lamp lit in a distant farmhouse. A thought crossed Frankl's mind, *Et lux in tenebris lucet*. "And the light shineth in the darkness." That bit of light signaled a life outside the brutal, seemingly meaningless world of the camp. "I sensed my spirit piercing through the enveloping gloom," Frankl wrote. "From somewhere I heard a victorious 'Yes' in answer to my question of the existence of an ultimate purpose."

Though the people who lived in the house might rightly be considered "the enemy," Frankl chose to focus on what connected him to these strangers: their common humanity. Frankl's distant lamp is a bit like the glimpses we see into the houses of strangers from a passing train. Both offer hope that we share far more than what separates us.

GOD, THE MANIFEST

Cleared fields, leafless trees:
what lay hidden all summer
made bare — barn, bridge, bird

J V

The two-and-a half-hour drive between my home in central Illinois and the city of Chicago, where I frequently work, often telescopes for me the passage of time through the seasons. Sometimes the shifts are dramatic, as in winter. Through the bare trees, I can detect things once concealed by foliage: a barn, a bridge, a bird's nest tucked between branches. One day I noticed so many new sights, I felt as though I was traveling an unfamiliar road, even though the drive was completely routine.

And yet, I miss so much of what exists. I don't see it because I'm not paying attention. The same is true in other parts of my life. I miss the good qualities in a person simply because I'm not looking for them. In his memoir *Drama: The Education of an Actor*, John Lithgow describes the qualities necessary for exceptional acting. "One of the most basic things an actor must learn," he says, "is that human beings are capable of anything. Each and every one of us can be noble, courageous and kind. But we can also be cowardly, cruel and contemptible. All of those qualities, good and bad, can often erupt from nowhere when you least expect them in the least likely people. Good people can do terrible things, bad people can astonish us with their goodness."

When I pay closer attention to a person or a situation, I often uncover a hidden reality. It is similar to the way I see the landscape more accurately in winter, when the brush has cleared and the trees have lost their leaves. Then I can sense the real behind the real.

GOD, THE WATCHER

Pink message slip floats
to pavement from higher place:
words from where, to whom?

JV

It's often easier for me to be "contemplative" when I'm in a relaxed setting — on vacation, say, or during a spiritual retreat. But I've learned that with enough practice, even a traffic-choked street in the center of a large city can lead to moments of contemplation.

Standing at a bus stop one day, instead of tuning out as I often do, I remained alert to the scene around me. A man in a cashmere coat carrying a leather briefcase stopped to give some cash to a homeless man sitting on a crate. What struck me was that the businessman didn't walk away immediately, as I expected him to. He spent a few minutes conversing with the homeless man. As I watched this encounter, a pink message slip floated down on the pavement in front of me. It might have slipped out of someone's satchel or fallen from a window in one of the nearby office towers. I thought of all the people ensconced in their cubicles inside those towers. I thought of the person who sent the message and the person for whom the slip of paper was meant, who might now never receive its message.

In her book *Long Quiet Highway: Waking Up in America*, Natalie Goldberg writes of watching her beloved Zen teacher wait at a curbside for his ride to arrive. When the teacher receives word that his driver is running late, he doesn't appear worried or impatient. He simply nods and says, "Thank you." Goldberg recalls, "Until I saw that kind of equanimity, I didn't think it was possible." She later told a friend. "I saw him standing outside." What was he doing while he was standing, the friend wanted to know. "Nothing … He was standing," Goldberg replied. Same as I was doing that day at the bus stop. Nothing. Which felt a lot like contemplation.

GOD, THE ENRICHER

My birth date arrives,
no blinding light stuns. Dawn comes,
just dawn, and enough

J V

My birthday, January 25, falls in the Catholic liturgical calendar on the Feast of the Conversion of St. Paul. For much of my life, that meant very little to me. With his harsh pronouncements on women and sexuality, Paul was not a particular favorite of mine. But as I grow older, I appreciate more the necessity of occasionally being knocked off my high horse as Paul reportedly was.

As Scripture tells it, Paul, despiser of Christians, was en route to Damascus when he heard the voice of Jesus say, "Why do you persecute me?" He was so stunned by whatever apparition he saw, that he fell to the ground from his horse and a period of physical blindness followed. He eventually not only regained his sight, but from then on approached life with a new way of seeing. In spite of his personal shortcomings, or perhaps because of them, he was able to write some of the most poetic and affecting passages of the New Testament. He traveled the far corners of the ancient world, preaching a message of hope and mercy. *For now we see through a mirror darkly, but one day we will see face to face … Though I speak with the tongues of men and of angels and have not love, I am but a sounding brass or clanging cymbal … Love is patient, love is kind. Love bears all things, hopes all things.*

Like Paul, I am grateful for the times I have fallen from a pinnacle of certainty and been forced to change how I think and how I see. Those experiences usually fill me with greater gratitude for the life I'm living, the love that I have and for the things, despite my considerable flaws, I have managed to accomplish. A favorite word of mine these days is *enough*. To be alive is simply enough.

GOD, THE RESTRAINER

Snow paints cars, streets, trees
What to do with so much white?
Sit still with no mind

J V

The Buddhist concept of *no mind* involves clearing the head of worry — of fears for the future and the useless rehashing of the past. *No mind* asks us to focus on the present moment.

Most years I dread the coming of winter, with its shorter hours of daylight, travel difficulties and cumbersome layers of clothing. But the more I age, the more I recognize the subtle beauty in this season. Winter encourages us to settle down. The necessity of spending more time indoors invites us to look inward and reconnect with what's essential. In the Christian tradition, winter spans the liturgical seasons of Advent and Lent. Both are times for sweeping out the dust that's accumulated in our psyche over the course of a year.

Now, instead of dreading the first frost, I welcome it. I look forward to days of quiet reading in a warmed room, to steaming cups of afternoon tea, to deeper darknesses that allow me to appreciate even more the fewer daylight hours and the nights lit by a full moon. It is the perfect season to cleanse the mind.

GOD, THE SUBDUER

Irate man curses
woman's driving. She calls back
God bless you, drives on

J V

Japanese haiku have a long association with nature poetry. Classical haiku usually mention a specific season. In the city, with its limited access to nature, I take my haiku where I find them. Often they come to me when I'm driving.

Road rage just may be the stupidest expenditure of emotion. Yet, I can hardly say I'm immune to it. I get angry at drivers who cut me off, speed up alongside me as I'm trying to change lanes, or wait until the last minute to put on their turn signal. Once, I unleashed a series of profanities at a driver who nearly hit my car, only to realize seconds later it was a parish priest I know.

That's why this woman's compassionate reaction to a male driver's impatience remained with me long after I witnessed the incident. Some things just aren't worth the energy it takes to get angry. It's much easier on the psyche — and the soul — to offer a blessing and drive on.

GOD, THE LIVING

In yellowed journals
they work, love, argue, complain:
those long dead, live

J V

I never knew my husband's mother, Helen Rizzoli Reynard. But one day, rummaging around the cellar, my husband unearthed a set of her diaries. Suddenly, I was able to enter the life of this dedicated mom who worked the night shift as a registered nurse. Her entries, sometimes recorded in leather-bound journals, at other times in inexpensive spiral notebooks, span the years from 1953 until 1985, when she became too debilitated by Alzheimers to write. She often crystallized in a few terse sentences an entire day.

A typical entry might read, "Today I went to Galyan's and bought a cut-up chicken on sale, then on to the yarn store but couldn't find the green color I wanted." Then a few days later: "A man was admitted to the ward last night with congestive heart failure. He'll probably die here. His young, inexperienced doctor doesn't know which end is up." She records the day President Kennedy was assassinated and the morning her second husband collapsed and died of a stroke on their front porch while she and her son were at church. She writes of having her gall bladder removed and her disappointment at being turned away from a dance class because she didn't have a partner.

In these journals, the mother-in-law I never knew lives again. Through them, my husband can reconnect with grandparents, aunts and uncles long gone, memories long faded. His mother's journals are proof that no life is "ordinary." Each day is its own feature film worthy of being preserved.

GOD, THE DESIGNER

Neutrons seek protons
they hold the world together
for what, if not love?

JV

There is a wonderful book by Bill Bryson called *A Short History of Nearly Everything*. It describes how the universe probably formed, how cells work, how electronic waves and particles were discovered, and what goes on still today beneath the earth's surface.

What I found most intriguing, though, is how all things, from protons to planets, collaborate, like the components of a perfectly calibrated watch. A few degrees hotter and the inner core of the earth would explode. A few milliseconds farther from the sun, and we earthlings wouldn't have to worry about getting around in fossil-fueled vehicles, we'd be cross-country skiing everywhere on a planet of permanent arctic tundra.

Scientists and theologians, believers and agnostics, can argue whether an intelligent design — the work of a divine mastermind — lies behind such precision. I like to fantasize that it is the universe's love for us that holds things together in such a delicate balance. All the universe seems to ask in return is that we care for it and one another.

GOD, THE WISE

Words eluded me
lifted like tails of white deer
fleeing through dense woods.

PQ

One morning as I wandered the fields around the abbey where I live in a dim winter light, I suddenly sensed the ghost-like appearance of wildlife. A deer perhaps. It was a vision as noiseless and swift as the mind itself. I followed the vision's movement, tramped clumsily over tree fall and brush.

In a similar way, I often stumble onto old regions of memory, a tour that takes me to places long abandoned and life in locations left far behind. When I walk through the woods, my clambering and crouching to avoid thorny shrubs and low-hanging branches conditions my body. But it also conditions my mind. I twist along tracks of self-knowledge and venture into strange or new areas. I might rediscover an old grove, grown wilder and more unfamiliar and wonder why I left it unvisited for so long. At the same time, I make forays into old ground and barely recognizable slopes of my past.

Writing itself can be an ordeal of trying to catch up with what has long escaped me, or of recognizing at last that something of the past will remain impossibly out of my reach. Best sometimes just to leave it at that, not write at all, and let silence honor the knowledge and memories that elude me.

GOD, THE STRAIGHTENER

"Narrow is the way"
How narrow? Tight as the vent
babes squeeze through at birth

PQ

This huge planet, composed of small things, is endlessly rich and delightfully curious to our tiny world of haiku. We might view life as an exercise in finding smaller and smaller gates to pass through in order to discover the grand scale of things. Haiku develops an eye for detail as it opens a door to beauty. Beauty is never too small for the beholder. Beauty has no measure.

"Your Father in heaven," Jesus tells us, "knows every sparrow that drops to the ground."

If nothing is too small for the creator of all being, should anything be too small for me? Perhaps in the end the most difficult and narrow passage one takes in life is through that most singular thing of all — through the one and only being that is *myself*. I am the narrow gate and must strip myself of all pretenses of being someone else. Every last item of baggage, every belt or shoe dropped and abandoned — even my claims to simplicity, integrity and poverty — must ultimately go.

The one thing remaining is to be myself, alone, and to emerge as none other.

GOD, THE ALL-HEARING

Snow crunch underfoot
groans up through leg bones to ears
complaining of cold.

PQ

GOD, THE BRINGER OF DISHONOR

Distant barking dog
carries on fierce argument
with dull, heedless world.

PQ

It is said that when St. Bernard of Clairvaux's mother was about to give birth to her son, she dreamed of a barking dog. She was told her dream meant that a prophet was about to be born. I am not sure why a barking dog symbolizes a prophet, unless it is because prophets tend to be a nuisance, particularly to the complacent.

In the vicinity of the abbey where I live, it seems we have many canine prophets. Hearing the persistent tone of some, I am left thinking how frustrating life must be for anyone given to telling the truth to an unheeding public.

A prophet is rarely accepted in his own country, Jesus warned. Neither sometimes is a dog in his own neighborhood.

GOD, THE UNMANIFEST

Barely audible
wind in firs — old earth, Great Beast
breathing in deep sleep

PQ

Sometimes Earth seems to me to be a great cosmic beast, one whose presence you sense through its pervasive scent. Like a beast, Earth is something alien and unpredictable, a life largely unknown to us. It sets a track of its own that we must follow to survive or else perish.

Some prefer to think of eErth as Mother, one who knows what her children want. But Earth can also be feral, dangerous and hostile to our wants. When Earth quakes, the native Pacific Islanders say a turtle moved, for they believe the planet rests on a turtle. But a turtle is cold-blooded.

I prefer to see Earth as a warm-blooded creature, wild, unpredictable — an animal like us, yet mostly unseen and more reclusive, breathing with the wind.

GOD, THE PURE

Peace came to my door
Without luggage or sandals
With just its name — peace

PQ

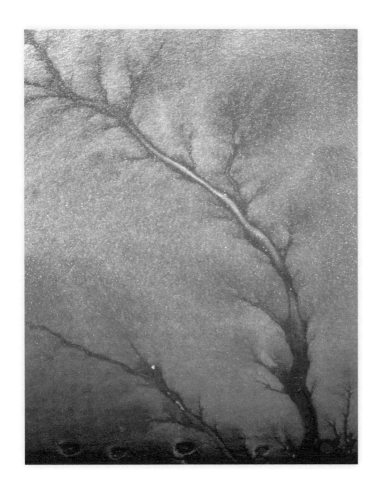

GOD, THE STRONG

Night winds prowled about,
grabbed loose shambles to buffet,
rattle and tumble

PQ

Sleeping outside under a porch roof as I regularly do, makes for poor rest when a fierce wind whips up. I might retreat indoors or meekly decide to tolerate the storm. Or I might brace up and take on the wind as if it were a tough character with rough manners — a tad difficult, but not impossible to befriend.

Last night the wind beat my sleeping bag's hood against my ears, overturned a chair and flung one of my pillows onto the grass. I scooted my mattress snug against the outer wall of the lumber shed, seeking greater shelter, and persevered, mesmerized by the prowling performance.

Sometimes it is just simpler to make a friend of adversity.

GOD, THE SUBLIME

All was silent 'til
dove sang morning homage to
sun at earth's far rim

PQ

In cooler weather, the appearance of the first crest of direct sunlight on the horizon corresponds closely to the beginning of bird song. If I a bird starts to sing before the light, it is because he or she is perched high in a tree and can see the bright curve before I can. I like to think that the sun is the closest thing to God birds can fathom. They rejoice to announce the sun's appearance, as if it marks a miracle in their day.

Scientists have discovered that birds' eyes contain an extra cone beyond the three that we and other mammals have. Birds see colors we can't because their eyes absorb a wider range of light waves.

And while I'm at it — how is it that such a great volume of sound comes out of such a small creature? Perhaps science will one day uncover the answer. Meanwhile, suffice it for us to appreciate the sound — and colors of the day — as only the human can, even with the limited and unbirdlike range of our senses.

GOD, THE JUDGE

One ice patch in town
Big enough to make her slip
She just had to laugh

MB

Ice-covered streets and sidewalks are rare sights indeed in southern California. But one winter morning it was cold enough outside to freeze water that had seeped out of a lawn irrigator. A rogue patch of ice formed on a stretch of pavement. It was perhaps the only piece of black ice ever recorded in the history of Claremont, California!

A dear friend on her way to work, rushing along a familiar and pleasant path, discovered the slippery patch too late with her heel. She went down swiftly and all the way. Lying on her rump, the contents of her purse, her iPhone and work documents scattered around her, she had to laugh.

Was it divine judgment or comedy that visited her? Or perhaps was that unexpected pause in her morning a sign of grace?

GOD, THE SUPERIOR

Quest for perfection
Chipped teacup with rambling cracks
My scarred leather boots

                                        M B

An old Japanese proverb says, "Perfection is a chipped tea cup." It recalls the impulse that drove ancient Japanese and Chinese artists to leave a small flaw in each of their works to avoid angering the God-force of the universe, the seat of all perfection.

The philosophy of *wabi sabi* urges us to seek the beauty in flaws, the way the starkness of winter forces us to look more deeply for beauty. The path of haiku invites us to find sacredness right where we stand, sit, walk, eat and sleep, even in faults and deficiencies.

All we need do is open our eyes and see with the soul.

GOD, ALL OF LIFE

Flash of memory
Unconditional lover
Streak of gold in snow

MB

To have loved and lost a great animal is to open ourselves to the mystery of relationship. My dog Daisy was a mixture of husky, beagle and chow. She and I spent many days alone in wilderness. I loved to watch her lope across snowy fields, spring blossoms and autumn leaves. Such unbounded ecstasy! Such exhilarating passion!

When I was recovering from heart surgery, she would lie as close to me as she could and purr deeply. We were both, Daisy and I, ailing in her last days. We lay together long nights and days, transfusing strength one to another. She did not want to leave me, nor I her, even when a peaceful death seemed the best possible blessing she could still receive.

Sometimes when I see a spot of sun streaming into a room from the window, I sense Daisy's presence. She was like that, a streak of gold.

GOD, THE ALL-EMBRACING VASTNESS

Morning star rises
True enlightenment
Reality unclothed

MB

Zen practitioners often speak of the proverbial "finger pointing to the moon." The finger points to something *beyond*. The finger must not be mistaken for the moon. Nor should what the Tibetan tulku Chogym Trungpa has labeled *spiritual lust* be mistaken for enlightenment. Spiritual lust is the extreme desire for spiritual "experiences." We bounce from event to event, like someone lost in a dark room frantic to find the light switch. It can turn into just another form of ego gratification.

The Buddha is said to have found enlightenment, not by striving for it (though he initially did a fair amount of that), but only by becoming still at last. It was then he saw the rising of the morning star and all reality opened to him. He felt he had found the gate to heaven.

On a rare visit outside his cloister, the great Trappist monk Thomas Merton stood on a busy corner in the middle of downtown Louisville. He felt there an overwhelming sense of the sacred. And like the Buddha, he entered into a deeper reality. "I was suddenly overwhelmed with the realization that I loved all these people, that they were mine and I theirs, that we could not be alien to one another even though we were total strangers," he wrote later in his journal. "There is no way of telling people that they are all walking around shining like the sun ... I have no program for this seeing. It is only given. But the gate of heaven is everywhere." No need to lust after it.

GOD, THE RIGHTEOUS TEACHER

Incense, cold front porch
Ancestors sigh in high steam
Sanctum sanctorum

MB

Heȟáka Sápa was an Oglala Sioux holy man whose name means Black Elk. He lived in wholeness and holiness in an industrial world his forebears could not have imagined. Yet, he remained true to his people, his ancestors and his vision. He listened to his spirit voice and continued singing his traditional songs in a strange land.

Black Elk married a Catholic woman and was eventually baptized a Catholic, as were their children. He even became a missionary to the very people who blasphemed his ancestors and ultimately eradicated their way of life. Still, he considered all Christians his people too. He served as a catechist until his death in 1950, finding no apparent contradiction between this work and his faithfulness to his ancestors. Coming down from a mountain where he had received a vision of the future for both Native Americans and their conquerors, he proclaimed that "Everywhere is the Holy Land."

Everywhere. Even a cold front porch on a rainy Sunday morning can become a chapel of the heart.

GOD, THE ALL-FORGIVING

Holy fools we are
Alive and lost in Eden
Loving excrement

MB

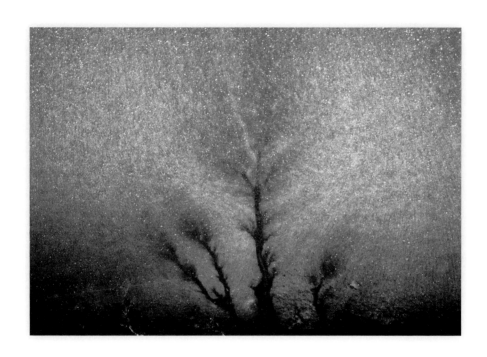

GOD, THE GREAT

Sun shines in darkness
Creation's open secret
Never extinguished

MB

The Inuits of the frozen North believe that even the long nights of winter contain the seeds of light. Those who have been fortunate enough to have had a good hunt and have survived the winter sing a song that expresses the radical faith of those whose existence depends on beliefs stronger than dogma:

> *I think over again my small adventure,*
> *My fears, those small ones that seemed so big,*
> *For all the vital things I had to get and reach.*
> *And yet there is only one great thing,*
> *The only thing,*
> *To live to see the great day dawn*
> *And the light that fills the world.*

In the small adventures that are our individual lives, night fears can cling to us like sweat-soaked clothes. But there is an unseen reality. We find it when "the great day dawns," when we can start anew. The filmmaker Frances Hubbard Flaherty once wrote, "As ice turns to water and water to steam, and a degree of temperature becomes a transformation, so a degree of seeing may become a transformation." Sometimes all it takes is to look at a thing askance.

GOD, THE PATRON

Midnight reverie
Yet silently unobserved
Oak falls in Bangkok

MB

The year 1968 was a time of monumental sadness and upheaval. The Vietnam War entered one of its bloodiest phases. Martin Luther King and Robert Kennedy were felled by assassin's bullets and on December 10 of that year, Thomas Merton, one of the greatest spiritual teachers of the twentieth century, died on a visit to Bangkok. It took a freak accident to down this towering giant. Stepping out of the shower, Merton touched a high voltage fan and was immediately electrocuted.

The following day, December 11, was momentous to me for a far more mundane reason. It was my twenty-first birthday. With an exhilarating blast of freedom, I joined the cult of adulthood with a celebration that began at midnight. But a tree had fallen in the woods halfway around the world. And I did not hear it.

Nonetheless, the felling of that mighty oak was to reverberate in my life in the years to come in many and mysterious ways. I would become a student of Merton's words long after his death. When an event occurs in life, we may not at first take note. But a great while later, it may begin to resound, like a ringing in the ears.

GOD, THE EVER-RELENTIING

Relentless deadlines
Scent of fresh flowers fills air
I mustn't miss this spring!

JV

When I reported for *The Wall Street Journal*, I had a desk near a window on the 21st floor of the newspaper's Chicago bureau. Most mornings I'd arrived at nine and bury my head in my work. At some point, I'd look out the window and realize that it had grown dark outside. The day had passed and I'd missed it!

One reason I love spending time at monasteries is that monastic men and women honor the rhythms particular to each part of the day. They do this by pausing regularly for prayer. Vigils before dawn. Lauds at sunrise. Terce in early morning. Sext at the half point of the day. None in mid-afternoon, Vespers in the early evening and Compline to complete the day. To mark the hours this way fills me a sense of having *lived* each day. Similarly, monastic life celebrates the richness of each season. I find it is much harder to maintain this type of heightened awareness over the passage of time within the bustle of a normal work day. It requires a conscious effort.

When I am working, I have to force myself to pause periodically, to become aware of the passing hours. In a poem called "Eyesight," the poet A.R. Ammons writes about missing the first buds of spring in the place where he lives. He travels farther north to where the trees have not yet blossomed, hoping for a second chance at experiencing the initial blush of the season. But make no mistake, the poet warns, *it's not that way/with all things, some/ that go are gone.*

GOD, THE SUBTLE AND PROFOUND

No thought, only pond
No mind, only insect's buzz
No ache, only breath

JV

Whenever I visit the Abbey of Gethsemani, I try always to take a long late afternoon walk around the grounds with my friend Brother Paul Quenon. We hike across alfalfa fields, pass sassafras trees and cypresses, and often end our trek by resting on the flat rocks alongside one of the abbey's many ponds. We remain quite still, marveling at how, in late afternoon, the moon shows itself on the tranquil surface of the water. When we begin our march back to the monastery, we often walk in silence. There is a bridge over one of the ponds where Brother Paul likes to pause long enough to recite from memory a poem by Wendell Berry from a collection called *Given*. Berry describes coming to a place of water and light, of birds singing and leaves in shadow. After years of familiarity, he feels so connected to this site that both the outside world and his inner world there merge into one. There are no longer *thoughts of these/but they are themselves/your thoughts*.

Berry's poem is as apt a description as any of true contemplation. We live in the *continuous mystery of now*, my Benedictine friend, Abbot Owen Purcell, likes to say. The Buddhists talk about living mindfully. The Benedictines call it living "intentionally," recognizing that there is meaning in every activity, as Abbot Owen tried to describe in a short poem he wrote:

> *I've never been where I am not*
> *I've always been where I am*
> *Goodbye to the past that was now*
> *Hello to the now that I'm in.*

GOD, THE ADVANCER

We forgo hour's sleep
for extra moment of light
Bead hung on day's end

J V

Daylight saving time is our man-made device for cheating nature in order to squeeze into our days an extra hour of light. Of course, we repay the debt the following fall when we turn our clocks back again to standard time. If you travel east to west on a flight, say from Chicago to Maui, you end up reliving the same hours you left behind. Depending on when you travel, you may see one continuous sunset spread over the course of many hours. On such flights, I have the sense of adding time to my life. It's of course an illusion, but I like to fantasize that if I traveled far enough without turning back again, I could actually add an entire day to my life.

I often wish I could repeat certain days — my wedding day, for instance, or a day when I argued with someone I love and now wish I had the chance to behave differently. I would like, too, to relive the final times I saw both my parents alive. At least then I would have known it was to be the last time.

In Thornton Wilder's *Our Town*, young Emily Webb is allowed to return from the dead to relive a single day of her choosing. She swiftly discovers how much time the living waste lost in "ignorance and blindness." Unlike Emily, I won't be able to return from the dead some day to set the ledger right. The only course of action I have is to live well the day at hand, the only time I have to live it.

GOD, THE GLORIOUS

Peonies so bold
in pink, seem to be calling
Look at me, ME!

JV

The French have an amusing expression to describe people who call attention to themselves wherever they go. They are referred to as *"moi tu as vu,"* literally, "Have you seen me?"

Our culture often rewards the person who stands out from the crowd and dismisses those with an unassuming presence. One of my best friends at Mount St. Scholastica Monastery in Atchison, Kansas, is Sister Thomasita Homan. Sister Thomasita seems to carry stillness with her wherever she goes. At first I thought it was because she is a naturally quiet person. But as I came to know her better, I realized that her stillness reflects a kind of humility. Humility isn't a topic you'll find lining the bookshelves of Barnes & Noble. But it is the subject of the longest chapter in *The Rule of St. Benedict*, the essential guide to monastic living. Humility isn't the same as humiliation. Its Latin root is *humus*, which means "of the earth." St. Benedict placed humility at the heart of the spiritual quest. It isn't about diminishing ourselves, but rather about standing still in the midst of our common humanity. In a gesture I find so moving, the sisters at Mount St. Scholastica bow to one another across an aisle before beginning their community prayer. It is a way of saying, "I recognize the sacred in you; we are all in this together."

It is the nature of flowers, like the beautiful June peonies, to call attention to themselves. The challenge to us as human beings, St. Benedict says, is to be the first to show respect for another.

GOD, THE FRIEND

Day of solitude
Six wild turkeys come to stay
No one is alone

JV

Mother Teresa of Calcutta once identified what she called "the great American illness." It is not heart disease, diabetes or even cancer, she said. It is loneliness. When I was a young single woman starting my journalism career, I worked the kind of long hours that left little space for nurturing friendships, let alone any kind of romantic relationship. I'd arrive home at night to my studio apartment, heat up a can of Chef Boyardee ravioli for dinner and stare across the table at an empty chair. Hundreds of other people lived in the same high rise as I did. I could even peer into the sitting room of the people who lived in the building across the way. Yet I felt impossibly alone.

Some evenings I would sit on the edge of the bathtub, my head in my hands and weep, believing I would always feel this isolated. Perhaps it's a function of growing older, but I rarely feel such a crushing sense of loneliness anymore, even on days when my husband is away and I am at home alone. It could be that I'm more comfortable now being on my own, or perhaps I'm just more adept at looking for companionship. These days, I write in a cabin in the woods. I might well feel lonely except for the many creatures who arrive, unbidden, to share my day. Sometimes it's a doe and her faun. Other times a family of raccoons. Recently, a troupe of wild turkeys took up residence in our alfalfa field.

In the last three years of his life, the Trappist monk Thomas Merton lived as a hermit in a remote cabin on the grounds of his abbey. But he was rarely alone. Geese interrupted his prayer. And for a while he shared his outhouse with a pesky snake. "Are you in there, you bastard?" Merton would call, opening the outhouse door. Like Merton in his hermitage, I've learned that, on this planet brimming with life, no one is alone.

GOD, THE FASHIONER OF FORMS

Aircraft's vapor trail
leaves arched eyebrow over sky's
one unblinking eye

J V

When you live amid human construction in the heart of a city, as I have for much of my life, it's easy to feel detached from nature. And yet nature — God's construction — co-exists with humankind's. Stems of clover push through cracks in concrete sidewalks. Pots of geraniums and petunias hang over the iron balconies of downtown high rises. The sun's single eye remains unblinking as a Boeing 777 jetliner leaves behind a fantail of exhaust.

We can spray all the pesticides we want. We can slaughter any number of animals. We can build endless skyscrapers. But we will never completely subdue nature. We remain tenants in common on this planet with everything in the natural world. We are, at best, co-equals occupying communal real estate.

The next time I see a dog being walked on a leash on a city street, I will bow to it. When I walk through a park in the middle of an urban neighborhood, I will do the same for the tulips and the impatiens. When I look up at the faithful moon and sun, I will offer them too a nod of gratitude.

GOD, THE PROTECTOR

Sparrow lies injured
in street. I with my bag of
groceries, don't stop

JV

On my first trip to Mexico, a taxi took me from the airport to the resort city of Acapulco. An accident involving several cars had taken place along the route and injured passengers lay bleeding on the roadside. None of the cars ferrying passengers to the beachfront hotels stopped to offer assistance. When I suggested to my taxi driver that we pull over and help, he merely shrugged and kept driving. The tourist trade could not slow down for a few bleeding Mexicans.

I have never forgotten that scene. It should have been a lesson, but, here in the states, I often pass disabled cars on the roadside. And yet I'm too timid to stop, especially if I am traveling alone. There is perhaps good reason for a woman driving on her own to fear for her safety, but the truth is that most of the time, I'm simply in too much of a hurry to get where I'm going. Most people have cell phones, I rationalize. They can call for help.

One day as I walked home from the grocery story, I spotted an injured sparrow lying on the sidewalk near my home. But with a load of groceries in my arms, I didn't feel like stopping to investigate. When I returned a while later, the sparrow had died. I thought of the Samaritan traveler who went out of his way to save the life of a wounded stranger. I doubt I could have saved that sparrow. All I could do was give it a quiet burial, which, to this day, still haunts me as far too little.

GOD, THE COMPELLER

Outside before daylight,
rabbit senses foe, scampers,
made old by much fear

JV

One morning before daylight, I went outside to walk our aging dachshund. A young rabbit sat motionless on our neighbor's lawn. It sensed the presence of two alien creatures and quickly darted away. Neither the dog nor I meant it any harm, yet the rabbit sized us up and judged us to be adversaries.

I think of how many times I've wrongly ascribed the worst of motives to others. I think, too, of the times I hesitated to do something — take swimming lessons, propose an idea, travel to a new country, initiate a relationship — out of fear. I've wasted countless hours fretting over events that hadn't even happened yet.

Thomas Merton had a term for this: useless worry. Our neighborhood rabbit probably had more reason to fear my elderly dog and me than I've had to panic over so many things that turned out to be nothing more than useless worries. Today I vow to face the world with eyes that see and expect only good. I do not want to grow old with fear.

GOD, THE KIND

Warm, humid night breeze:
air is wafting with skunk love
— enough for us all.

PQ

Skunks do not deserve their bad reputation, at least not the ones I've encountered. From a distance, their scent is pungent rather than offensive. It serves to attract a mate, not to be used as a defense weapon.

Particularly in the month of February, skunk romance is in the air. On some nights, they court each other with a sing-songy meow. If you happen to meet one at night in the yard, it will approach, curious and tame as a kitten. I back away anyhow.

I understand that some find even the distant smell of skunk disagreeable. I do not claim it is appealing, but it does serve to remind me that the world is not ours alone. Perhaps skunks think they are showing kindness to include humans in their tender, blissful moods, putting their romance — and their scent — out there into the atmosphere. If so, who can begrudge them?

GOD, THE PRESERVER

It is not a weed,
it's a misplaced plant, he said
Let's leave it misplaced

PQ

The late Brother Harold Thibideau earned a degree in horticulture before he entered the Abbey of Gethsemani. He could answer any question anyone might pose about flowers. He had an affinity for Buddhist spirituality and often approached situations with a phlegmatic, Zen-like attitude.

Once, when someone complained about a stubborn weed in the flowerbed, his reply was "It's not a weed, it's a misplaced plant." His response pretty much encapsulated his stance toward the universe.

Eventually that "weed" grew to be a tall, stately mullein that nicely marked the foreground of a distant set of hills — a wonder sprung from Brother Harold's attitude of "live and let live."

GOD, THE ETERNAL

Stepping stones of time —
mere waves — we walk on water
'til ocean is gone

PQ

GOD, THE SELF-SUBSISTING

Simple, unseen bird
repeats with satisfaction
being here, here, here

PQ

In his characteristically laconic verse, the poet Robert Lax once wrote, *What bliss to be one of the beings.* Common birds like sparrows, finches and starlings offer characteristically unglamorous song repertoires, but who's to deny that they just might be communicating what is most important to us all.

Prayer is not measured by wordiness, or subtlety of thought, or range of feeling, but by simplicity and presence. Common sparrows are happy enough being one of the beings without having much else to declare about it.

So too the one who prays in silence.

GOD, THE LIBERATOR

Warm, moist, soft, soothing —
So much kindness in this breeze
— unknown saint perished?

PQ

There are many stories from ancient times about how a monastery would fill with a pleasant scent when a holy monk died. They called it the odor of sanctity.

My former Abbot, Father Flavian Burns, often said that real saints remain mostly unknown. We will not know who they were until we enter heaven.

Meanwhile, what do we know of saints? Is there something perceived but unseen in the benign weather that possesses us with its charm? Who can say that the wind has not blown our way a holy soul released from its body, from somewhere nearby or afar?

GOD, THE RESPONDER

Smart Mockingbird learned
to mimic my alarm clock
Woke me twice last night

PQ

Though we monks are afforded small, spare private bedrooms within the abbey, for many years now I have preferred to sleep at night in the open air. I use a bare mattress for my bed within the shelter of an outdoor wood shed.

To avoid being late for our first prayers of the day, I usually keep an alarm clock by my side. Suddenly awakened one night, I reached out to silence the alarm, then realized the sound was coming from the opposite direction. This later happened again. In my drowsiness, I finally figured out it wasn't my alarm clock at all, but a mockingbird's call. "Fool me once," the saying goes, "and you are the fool. Fool me twice and I am the fool." Apparently my winged neighbor does not mind playing the fool. He has made a career of that — or at least he tries. The other birds don't seem to be taken in by his perfect imitations of their diverse calls. He rarely succeeds at keeping them at bay.

I eventually concluded that my mockingbird friend, a light sleeper, merely wants attention as much during the night as he obviously does during the day. If I quietly talk back to him and courteously acknowledge his presence, using a few words and grunts, he will quiet down. We can rest contented knowing we are both there — I on my mattress, he in his tree. Nature loves familiarity.

GOD, THE ABUNDANT

Loopy night friends flit,
circle my desk lamp — mad moths,
imps and fairies all

PQ

I don't keep a screen on my window, and at night my reading lamp is the only light in the room. Moths and many curious winged things arrive and provide endless entertainment as I peruse Scripture. One of these creatures looks like a giant mosquito and is called a weaver bug. It does just that, randomly weaves about and hangs on the lampshade by one foot like a street drunk clinging to a lamp post.

St. Augustine took it as a mark of original sin that he could be so easily distracted from sacred reading by an insect. I take it as a sign of grace that something so small and comic can suddenly invade my solitude. Distraction it is, but my concentration is not to be coveted exclusively as a personal possession.

It is perfectly all right, as far as I am concerned, for God to shift my mind's mode to a brighter tonality and a smaller part of the universe.

GOD, THE SHAPER OF BEAUTY

Plum blossoms astir
Lingering pale afternoon
Intimate with day

MB

Dogen Eihei was a thirteenth-century Zen philospher. While his writing style may seem obscure to twenty-first century readers, his message still resounds. Eihei advocated slowing down, listening to what we see and watching what we hear. He called it seeing with a "third eye," the eye of contemplation.

His writing often reads like an extended haiku of many syllables. He once wrote, "At this moment of a single blossom there are three, four, and five blossoms, hundreds, thousands, myriads, billions of blossoms, countless blossoms, [for] blossoming is the old plum tree's offering."

It is the nature of plum blossoms to blow in the springtime breeze. From whence do they come and where do they go? Who knows? We are told by the wise that we can rest in the mystery of it, even as the flower fades. The questions are more important than the answers.

GOD, THE ALL-POWERFUL

Girl waters flowers
Study of art in motion
Brush strokes in action

MB

Renoir's "Girl with a Watering Can" is a transcendent work of art. I have examined its brush strokes at length over many visits to the National Gallery of Art. The paint very nearly bursts off the canvas in an exuberant laud to life.

When I watch my five-year-old granddaughter Nora as she cares for our beds of azaleas, impatiens and irises, Renoir's paint strokes come back in a vision. They superimpose themselves on the picture of my granddaughter bent over her patient, careful work.

Though one is a vision of art, and the other of life, both proclaim the perpetual renewal of all that is.

GOD, THE ORIGINATOR

Day candle ablaze
Shines light on golden landscape
Pure Land dances free

MB

The haiku master Basho Matsuo wrote, "If you want to know the pine, go to the pine." Meaning: rather than merely rhapsodize on the beauty of a pine, go to the source.

Haiku is like that. It goes back all the way to the ultimate Source. We travel beyond language and arrive at a place in the spirit. Shin Buddhists call it the Pure Land, the place of "one-thought moment."

It is also like "the still point" of which T.S. Elliot writes in his poem *Burnt Norton*: "Except for the point, the still point, / There would be no dance." At the Source, there is only the dance. The practice of haiku will take us there.

GOD, THE GATHERER

Listening to birds
Speaking and singing birdsong
Gloria! Always

MB

I once attended a Sunday morning Pentecostal worship service in the gritty farm town of Alcazar, Cuba. The "church" was a former storefront where a throng of worshippers overflowed into the dusty street. Children leaned out of open windows listening to the robust gospel *musica*, as tambourines, drums and electric organ pulsated from the worship space. Joy filled the air.

My Spanish was so rusty and their dialect so foreign to me that I struggled to understand what was being said. But I did catch something the pastor remarked at the outset. "Everybody knows when a Pentecostal service begins," he said, "but God only knows when it will end."

After three hours of vigorous celebration in music, scripture and testimony, my friends and I stood at the back of the room. Two hundred people — children, young husbands and wives, old folks with crutches and canes — all lined up to hug us. Many had tears in their eyes. Each one said over and over, *Gloria a Dios!* Glory to God. They wanted us to know they were overjoyed that we had come, listened and entered into their worship. Though I had not understood much of what was spoken, I heard their message. Just as today, watching the magnificent birds in my front yard, I hear theirs.

GOD, THE VICTORIOUS

Propitious moment
Surgeon opens sacred space
White dove bursts through clouds

MB

Each year, my wife Rena and I look forward to our annual get-together with our friends Jon and Sue. When I checked with Jon recently for confirmation of our yearly date, he emailed back, "Last Friday, a tumor was found in Sue's head for which she is having surgery today. All is on hold for now."

That afternoon at Our Lady of the Assumption Church, I lit a candle for Sue and for Jon. As I walked out the sanctuary doors, a white dove soared above me. It ascended to a bright spot of blue above the trees. Auspicious? Perhaps. Propitious? Surely.

But for now, we wait. Sometimes waiting is the only possible response.

GOD, THE RESURRECTOR

Watching as she sleeps
Original innocence
Primordial peace

MB

The most overwhelming sense of peace I can remember did not come to me during meditation, contemplation or formal worship, as I might have expected. I experienced it the night my mother died. Her room seemed to glow with a particular light. I had heard her final breath end in a long silence, just as last notes of a beloved Chopin sonata, softly playing on a nearby CD player, had disappeared into the ether. What innocence, courage and serenity registered on her face and in her body!

After sitting quietly for few minutes holding her still warm hand, I went across the hall to where my wife Rena was sleeping. Rena and my mother wore the same expression. Both were asleep in a heavenly peace. After I gently woke Rena, we went into my mother's room and sat without speaking in that warm glow that seemed almost viscous and ever so still.

Who knew that death itself could be so ravishingly beautiful?

GOD, THE NOURISHER

Robin watches me
Watching it through closed window
We both fly away

MB

GOD, THE ALL-AWARE

Redbud branch in breeze
pale enticing afternoon
erases thinking

M B

Thomas Merton did more than perhaps any other spiritual writer of the twentieth century to advance our understanding of prayer. Merton experienced and appreciated many forms of prayer. He chanted the Psalms daily with his fellow monks. He recited the rosary and prayed the liturgy of the Catholic Mass.

But Merton came to understand that the deepest form of prayer needs no verbiage. The deepest prayer rests in the stillness of the heart and quietude of the mind, in what he called "the hidden ground of our being." He once wrote, "There is so much talking that goes on that is utterly useless. It is in the sky, the sea, the redwoods that you will find answers."

Merton believed that the truest answers emerge not merely in thinking, but in being. I am grateful for those lazy afternoons when I can slow down long enough to notice a redbud tree's branches swaying in the wind. A time of thinking about not thinking.

GOD, THE PATIENT

Cicada crawls up
side of building, brick by brick
no deadlines to meet

JV

Wherever I write, I like to aim my desk toward a window so I can glimpse the world outside. One day, as I sat typing at a Benedictine monastery in a room on the third floor, I spied a cicada climbing the side of the building. At the pace it was going, it probably would take a couple of hours to inch up just two bricks. The cicada didn't seem in a hurry. It progressed, bit by bit.

The Benedictine motto is *Ora et Labora*, pray and work. But Benedictines seem to know when it is time to quit both. They even dare to call leisure *holy*. Late one evening, seeing a light on in my room, the prioress of the monastery knocked on my door. She invited me to shut down my computer and join her and some visiting prioresses for a glass of wine and some snacks. Stupidly, I said no and kept right on working.

The Benedictine writer Macrina Wiederkehr urges us to pause several times a day during the course of our work to allow our souls to catch up with the rest of our lives. Or as the White Rabbit in "Alice in Wonderland" says, "Don't just do something, *stand there*." I admired that cicada for its leisurely pace. It forced me to pause in the midst of my work, and reminded me that pauses, just like work, can be sacred.

GOD, THE PROVIDER

Crying child on bus
Such grievance at existence
this fine summer day

JV

One summer day on a city bus, I sat across from a mother and her crying child. The little girl's shrieks formed an odd juxtaposition to the glorious summer weather. Though the mother tried to soothe her daughter, nothing seemed to work. How could this child be so sad on such a perfect day?

Then I thought of one of my mother's cousins. When she lived in Brooklyn, she complained the neighborhoods were too crowded. Eventually she moved to Staten Island, where the houses were farther apart. So were the supermarkets, and she soon grumbled about the long walks she had to take to the store. Some relatives invited her to move near them in Mobile, Alabama. and found her a comfortable rental home. Within a matter of days, she griped that the stores in Mobile were more expensive than in New York and the people in Mobile less friendly. It's probably safe to say my mother's cousin wouldn't be content anywhere.

The ancient Greeks defined happiness as the use of all one's talents in a life affording scope. They recognized that happiness isn't so much a function of circumstances as what we do with those circumstances. In other words, happiness is an inside job. A friend of mine tells the story of her grandfather who was diagnosed with a virulent type of cancer. Doctors gave him six months to live. The family decided to spare him the news, and the old man lived another ten years. "He didn't know he was supposed to die," my friend says, and so he didn't. If we keep telling ourselves we're miserable, chances are we will be. Luckily, the inverse is also true. And sometimes all it takes to be happy is to stop crying and step outside on a splendid summer day.

GOD, THE BRINGER OF HONOR

My husband, shirtless,
walks our dog at daybreak,
each one dawn-faithful

JV

Rituals are often associated with a religious context: the Catholic Mass and sacraments; the Japanese tea ceremony; the Sabbath candle-lighting service; the burning of incense in Hindu temples. But our lives consist of many more secular rituals, though we may not name them as such.

Working mainly out of my home as writer, I can pretty much set my own schedule. But I miss some of the routines I developed when I reported to a newsroom — buying the newspaper from the same street vendor, picking up lunch at a handful of carry-outs, encountering the same people every day at the bus stop.

My husband, who works as an Illinois Circuit Court Judge, wakes at 5 a.m. each day, even though he doesn't have to be in his courtroom until 8:45. He walks the dog, drinks a cup of coffee, reads the newspaper, checks the day's court schedule on his computer, then finally makes breakfast before taking his shower and dressing. When I began to ask him to do some household chores in those morning hours, he patiently explained that this is his time to "center" himself before facing the work day. These customs are important to him, though they might seem superfluous to me. He is right. Our personal rituals are holy. Blessed are those who honor them.

GOD, THE EQUALIZER

Some carry pollen
Some spin honey, some guard hive
Low-wage bees fan, fan

J V

A beehive is like a miniature factory. Individual working groups are responsible for different functions, like segments of an assembly line. Some bees spin the honey, some carry back food to the hive and some serve as security guards for the premises. I'm especially fascinated by the group whose labor it is to fan the other bees as they go about their work. They remind me of the many low-wage workers, a good number of them immigrants, who perform the essential tasks that under-gird so much of our economy.

In recent years, a movement to crack down on illegal immigrants has gained momentum. Protesters complain immigrants take jobs from Americans. But do they? As a counter-protest, immigrants in Chicago decided to stay home from work on the same day. Restaurant patrons waited longer for their food because there were fewer cooks. Professionals returned to their offices to find their waste baskets filled with trash from the night before. Drivers faced long lines at car washes. The immigrants proved their point.

Not long afterward, I reported a story for PBS-TV on how the Catholic Church in America is becoming increasingly Hispanic. Our camera crew arrived at a Latino parish on the west side of Chicago for the feast of Our Lady of Guadalupe. It was a snowy December morning; the church was packed, although the sun hadn't yet risen. When the service ended about two hours later, many of the parishioners went off to jobs in factories, restaurants and office buildings across the city. I felt fortunate to be among such faithful and hard-working people. Borders are an arbitrary political construct. Are we not citizens of the one planet in the same universe? Everyone has a role to play. I learned that from the bees.

GOD, THE EVERLASTING

Crowds saunter along
city streets, oblivious —
this rice paper life

JV

One summer afternoon, stuck in heavy traffic, I scanned the pedestrians strolling along Chicago's Michigan Avenue. Well-dressed women clutched Nordstrom shopping bags, office workers carried briefcases full of "important" papers, young mothers pushed baby strollers, and elderly couples gripped cardboard cups of coffee as they window shopped. It was a continuous river of humanity. The more closely I observed their steps and their faces, the more they began to look to me like rice paper figures that could be torn, crumpled and tossed by the wind at any moment.

As long as we can breathe and think and walk or even lift ourselves out of a chair, it's easy to imagine we're invincible. We live in the illusion that everything and everyone will last. In truth, impermanence accompanies our every step. "All meetings end in departures," a famous Buddhist writer once wrote. Or, as the Psalmist says, our lives are like the grasses — here today and tomorrow withered.

That afternoon, I saw my own life for the fragile contraption it is. I thought about how tenuously knit my personal world is. And I loved my life and all the people in it even more.

GOD, THE COMPASSIONATE

Gnats invade kitchen
I fight urge to swat them dead
There is no God but God

J V

I do much of my writing now in a cabin in the woods. Sometimes I feel as if I share space with a hundred non-paying renters: the flies, gnats, spiders, ants, bees, beetles and mosquitoes that manage to let themselves in.

I'm like a god towering over these insects, ready to pounce. Then I remember a Quaker friend, pulling back my hand as I raised it to crush an ant. If we are to practice non-violence, he explained, it must include every living thing.

I can't say I'm always that charitable, especially to the mosquito buzzing my ear in the middle of the night, or the wasp that circles my head as I work, flashing its stinger. But these days, I'm more likely to gather up a spider in a paper towel and toss it outside or shoo a fly out the door than I am to kill those creatures. Live and let live. As the Koran reminds us, there is no God but God.

GOD, THE FORBEARING

Scent of ham and eggs
wakes me from dream: I must go
somewhere far. No car

JV

In many spiritual texts, dreams are often bearers of important messages. While asleep, Samuel hears God's call to become a prophet. In a similar way, Joseph is directed to change his plans and marry Mary. The Magi, in a dream, are warned against returning to Herod after seeing the Christ child.

In my own life, dreams often serve as guideposts. When I feel under pressure to complete a writing project or am about to make a presentation, I often dream that I must drive somewhere far, but cannot remember where I parked my car. In another of my recurring dreams, I have a lead role in a play (usually it's a musical). But as I step out on stage, I realize I haven't memorized my lines and cannot carry a tune. Dreams like these usually signal that I need to slow down. I need to clear my head of anxiety and get on with my work.

Sometimes dreams have pointed to changes in my life before they even occurred. Several years ago, my then-fiancé and I broke off our engagement by mutual agreement. I thought I'd never find another partner and made up my mind to live happily as a single woman for the rest of my life. One night, I dreamt a man sat cross-legged alongside me. He wrapped his arms around me and invited me to rest my head on his shoulder. Compassion poured from this man. The trouble was, I didn't know who he was. In the dream, I couldn't see his face. A few weeks later, I met the man who would become my husband. One afternoon, as we sat across from each other, I told him of the grief I still felt over my mother's death that had occurred around the same time as my broken engagement. He put his arms around me and lay my head on his shoulder. I felt the same compassion coming from him that I'd experienced with the stranger in my dream. In an instant, I realized the identity of the man in the dream. Ever since then I've kept careful note of my dreams. Dreams can be messengers. I listen to them with reverence.

GOD, THE MANIFEST

Men's after-shave,
movie lines, pizza delivery
Friday: America

JV

Of all the days of the week, Fridays, especially Friday afternoons, unfold to a special rhythm. My childhood home was located on a major traffic route. On Fridays, drivers seemed more hurried to get to where they were going. School, by contrast, was more leisurely. One of my teachers would play the soundtrack of a different Broadway musical every Friday afternoon. Friday carries its own distinct rituals. Families get pizza delivered or go out for Chinese food. Downtown bars spill over into the street with workers unwinding from the rigors of the week. Friday is date night, movie night, a time for bachelors to splash on an extra dab of after-shave.

I had an interesting experience one Friday afternoon walking along what used to be Fourth and Walnut streets in Louisville (now Fourth and Muhammad Ali streets). On this corner, the great Trappist writer Thomas Merton experienced what has come to be known as his "Louisville epiphany." After observing the workday crowds lope past him, Merton was moved to write, "I suddenly realized I loved all these people. I was theirs and they were mine. It was like waking from a dream of spurious separateness." I always thought it interesting that the realization that we are all connected didn't come to Merton while he prayed in his abbey, or sat in one of the world's great cathedrals. It came to him on a city street in the course of an ordinary work day.

In Merton's time, Fourth and Walnut anchored a commercial district of locally-owned stores. Today, it's a neon haven for national franchises and chain restaurants. At one of them, T.G.I. Friday's, the sign out front says, "Where every day is Friday." As much as I love Fridays, I wouldn't want every day to feel like Friday. Much better to experience each day's particular and enchanting rhythm.

GOD, THE OPENER

Wooden footbridge spanned
waterless creek — steps stroked dry,
dim marimba notes.

PQ

When the writer Judith Valente and her husband Charles Reynard visited my monastery, we took an afternoon stroll through the woods. We set a mutual challenge to each return with a haiku about our excursion. Soon afterward, my steps across a short, narrow bridge created a brief musical beat, a suggestion of spare words hidden in the wooden planks.

Most poems do not come by willing them. They come spontaneously, and by surprise, to an attentive mind. Nevertheless, extending an invitation to write can trigger an unexpected unfolding that opens up what otherwise would have remained closed. Monastic obedience is based on a similar premise. Poetic inspiration, according to Rainer Maria Rilke, is an act of obedience to the present moment. A monk's practice of obedience is in fact an excellent conditioning for art — genuine art that does not merely indulge subjectivity but carefully tracks, word by word, the truth of what is present in the moment.

Like the sound of footsteps on a wooden bridge.

GOD, THE ALL KNOWING

Robin keeps chuckling
at that story he found so
wickedly funny

PQ

What can one make of the sound of birds?

Sometimes they seem to be talking more to themselves than to anyone or anything there about. They carry on some private, inner-bird disquisition, some preoccupation, some special affair of the bird world that prepossesses them. And then they will go on and on about it quite endlessly. Or perhaps they simply intend to amuse themselves. One can only guess, which is all right.

Their message is clear: only fools need to understand *everything*.

GOD, THE ILLUSTRIOUS

Poor exhausted monk
Worn down to sleep by efforts
To think grand thoughts

P Q

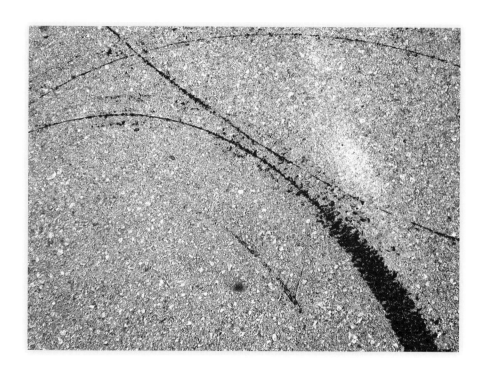

GOD, THE NUMBERER OF ALL

Lined straight up in row
fourteen bare feet on porch rest
firmly on one mind

PQ

A friend of mine, a jazz musician, recently converted his barn into a zendo, a kind of meditation hall. He calls it his "barndo." Occasionally he brings a group of men to the monastery where I live. They silently pace single file through the woods and up a hill. Their destination is the open air porch of Thomas Merton's hermitage. There, they sit and meditate. I call them the Ace Team Meditators.

Sitting shoeless, of course, and silent, all face a stretch of lawn that slopes off to distant ridge of hills, or knobs, as we in Kentucky say. Incense wafts through the air. An occasional bell or a recited text are the only human-made sounds that interrupt the quiet. It is a fine brew of camaraderie and concentration.

Filled with the calm of meditation, the group then heads to a nearby inn. There they share a different kind of Eucharistic cup, a few swigs of Kentucky bourbon, which serves as their concluding prayer of gratitude.

GOD, THE BESTOWER

Shrub overhung cliff —
branch reached deep in dense fog
seeking something lost.

P Q

Occasionally on my walks around the abbey, I am struck by the shape of a certain tree or shrub. Once it was a shrub over-hanging Monks Creek, which in its setting suggested to me infinite space. Another time it was a tree standing alone, found in no remarkable location. It could have been anywhere and nowhere, anonymous as time itself.

Such a singular tree, a fellow occupant of this common earth, makes a fine companion in solitude. After all, not every moment of enlightenment takes place under a Bodhi tree.

You too may have encountered such a plant or tree. Perhaps it had seemed ordinary, familiar and close to you all along. But when the stillness of early morning or the dim light and atmosphere of evening are just right, it can emit an aura of timelessness. Such a tree can remind us of our own place in the endless cycle of life.

GOD, THE CLEMENT

Rocking serenely
Chair keeps time with summer wind
Empty now yet wise

MB

On my porch at home is a large wicker chair with a soft green pillow seat. I take turns sitting in the chair with an unnamed friend: a stray cat that makes a bed there some nights.

A brisk breeze blows across the porch most days now. There is a companion chair on the porch, a wooden rocker that usually sits empty, but also sways gently in the wind. This aged rocker is somewhat of a mystery. When my mother died, we found it in her storage shed, with no back story at all. We can only guess its history, though it must be a rich one, given its apparent age and its many scuffs of time.

The rocking chair keeps its secrets. We cannot even be certain that its final home will be our front porch. For now, our tired chair seems content to sit quietly and rock, sharing its wisdom by example.

GOD, THE AVENGER

Wasp stinger hangs low
Is Wasp-being penance for
One life's aggression?

MB

If you believe in karma in the classical sense, you might imagine some people — or possibly even yourself — as a wasp in a previous life. Perhaps wasp-being is the karmic penance for having lived our human life poised to sting as we go.

One of the wasp's worst traits is its heedless aggression. It would just as soon sting a peach as a person. Why it chooses to stay and fight with stinger drawn in one instance, and simply buzz off without attack in another, remains a mystery of nature. The comeuppance is this: just one sting and it's lights out for our wasp friends.

As much as wasps tell us about insect nature, they can also teach us about our human tendencies, if we are paying attention. To return as a wasp or a star? If there is such a thing as karma, then the choice is ours.

GOD, THE LOVING

Crazy lovemaking
Green pastures beckon all day
Cloudless skies embrace

MB

The American naturalist John Muir once took up residence inside a tree. He said he wanted to experience the tree. Is this craziness or is it love? Perhaps we can say it is a little of both: crazy love. This is one definition of love: to be so intertwined with and in tune with another that we intuit the other's wholeness.

The great mystic St. Francis of Assisi came to see in birds, plants and animals, his brothers and sisters. He understood that to discover the wholeness of something is also to uncover its holiness.

John Muir recognized that to love profoundly is to be at one with the other and, in this way, to come to know the One. Or, as the Trappist Father Matthew Kelty once said, "The love of God is not different from the love of self or the love of the whole of creation. If you have the one, you have it all."

GOD, THE GIVER OF ALL

Orange bead hovers
Reigns over noontime sky
And soon there is night

MB

The ancient Chinese called their divining text, *I Ching: The Book of Changes*. The sun never sets on *The Book of Changes*; thousands of years after it was written, people around the world still plumb its wisdom. One finds there insights akin to those in the wisdom book of Ecclesiastes in Hebrew scripture. Both teach that nothing is new under the sun. And still, everything changes, turn, turn, turn, inevitable as the noonday sun or evening's darkness.

Es gibt was a favorite expression of philosopher Martin Heidegger. It means in German, "what is given," or "here it is." We are daily given dawn, daylight, twilight and darkness, but never in quite the same way.

As I sit on my porch on under a fiery noonday sun, I look forward to the peace of the coming night, the moon and stars that will soon flood the darkness with their glitter. Change is a constant. Tomorrow will come. *Es gibt.*

GOD, THE WITNESS

Three brief haiku lines
A sharp flash in the darkness
Just enough to see

MB

GOD, THE TREMENDOUS

Imperfect roses
Blossoms too red, thornless stems
One word: precisely

MB

GOD, THE MERCIFUL

Into the abyss
Evidence of caring hand
Signature of Love

MB

The Trappist writer Thomas Keating, has observed:

> *When all striving ceases*
> *I awaken to behold*
> *ever-present Awareness*
> *keeping silent watch*

When I emerged from emergency bypass surgery more than fifteen years ago, I awakened in many ways to a new life. I awoke, of course, to the harsh clinical lights of a hospital room. But in that bright fluorescent lighting, I sensed the palpable presence of a loving hand, and thought of something the poet/performer Leonard Cohen had written: "There's a crack in everything, that's how the light gets in." In that moment of altered, but supreme consciousness, I knew somehow that I had always lived in this splendid light and that I have always been loved. So has everyone else. That experience transformed me. Despite my own stubbornness, I became a person of faith.

John Caputo, the author of *Against Ethics*, has called faith "an art of construing shadows." A man or woman of faith, he says, "is not one who knows nothing of the abyss, but has looked down this abyss and construed it in terms of the traces and stirrings of a loving hand." Perhaps my awakening in that hospital room was just such a "construing," sealed with the signature of an invisible hand.

GOD, THE TRUSTWORTHY

Desolation ridge
Blind men, fools survive here
Amid stone graves

MB

In the Golan Heights of Israel, whole villages have been reduced to rubble. On a ridge overlooking Syria to the east and Lebanon to the north, I and a group of fellow travelers went tooling around on our own, against security rules. Four of us in a rented van. We hewed to the oil field roads until we came to Nameless City. It was literally a city with no name — pockmarked by bullet holes, its foundations bombed to ruins. Yet there was *something* there.

We stopped in the middle of the main street and gazed out over this ravaged village in silence. We walked a few yards and, one by one, entered what had been a home. There was no trace of humanity left, only hundreds of shell casings piled like so much garbage. And then we spotted it … a grenade, lying in a corner of what perhaps had been a kitchen floor. My friend reached to pick it up. Something rustled. A hawk flying by zoomed down low as if to warn us. My friend looked again at the grenade. It was live. The pin was still in it. We stepped away carefully, like a platoon in the jungle. Still shaken, we walked wordlessly back to our van.

One of us noticed a rusted sign lying in the rubble. It read (in three languages): EXTREME DANGER. THIS AREA IS MINED. DO NOT ENTER. Blind fools are sometimes mercifully protected amid stone graves.

GOD, THE EVOLVER

Meeting once again
Mystical recognition
Smooth stone in warm hand

MB

Our universe is an avid recycler. From the time of the "Big Bang" onward, the same atoms have cycled through space in various densities, formations and reformations. Nothing is ever lost in the countless recombination of particles. From rocks, oceans, animals and plants to homo sapiens, all things remain, even as they are transformed in a cosmic drama beyond human comprehension.

Perhaps that is why I felt a sense of life in the smooth white stone I picked up today and held in my hand. The cells in my hand met the untold thousands of dust particles that went into the creation of this rock millions of years ago. Atom meets atom from a distant past and knows. Thus, we sometimes find ourselves in a familiar place though we have never visited there before.

The ancient Israelites worshipped Yahweh, the unchanging God who superseded and transcended all ages. And yet Yahweh declares in the book of Isaiah, "Behold, I am doing a new thing. Do you not see it springing forth?" The dust from the dawn of creation flows down through the ages, still making all things new. Do we not see?

GOD, THE INHERITOR OF ALL

Heat sizzles soul
Inquisition of Spirit
Change in perception

MB

To arrive at the Benedictine monastery of Christ in the Desert near Abiquiu, New Mexico, you must leave the main highway and drive an hour or so along a sometimes impassable National Forest Service road. Eventually you will reach a canyon that has been inhabited by humans for at least 10,000 years. The first time I visited the monastery, there was one phone and almost no electricity, save for what solar panels provided. The panels were installed mainly to power the computers the monks use to create graphic art for websites, including that of the Vatican. That is how they earn their living. When it gets dark in the canyon, it grows very dark indeed, especially on cloudy nights or nights with a faint moon. After the dark womb of night, the sun also rises. It rose up a fiery red every day of my visit that July.

The artist Georgia O'Keeffe lived near Christ in the Desert. This was the light and landscape that had inspired her. From a narrow road just around the bend, one can see in the distance her beloved Pedernal, the hypnotic flat-topped flint mountain she painted often. The canyon is home to howling winds. Their presence has given rise to the myth of the Blue Witches, the apparitions of women in blue dresses said to arise at the top edge of the mesas when danger is near. The mysterious Penitente cult share this landscape along with the Benedictine monks in their peaceful little monastery. It is a spot that obviously holds many secrets. But what strikes me on every visit is how the admixture of silence, stark landscape, heat and light work a healing alchemy on mind, body and spirit.

Thomas Merton visited here once in 1968 a few weeks before he died. He asked O'Keeffe what she could see from here. "Only the whole world," she replied. A kindly monk from Christ in the Desert, welcoming me to my adobe cell, remarked, "You can't stay here two weeks without being changed." There are few places of which one can say the same. To find just one of them is pure gift.

GOD, THE ETERNAL

Pre-dawn silence
Earth murmurs ancient secrets
We listen, or not

J V

The ancient Celts viewed life as a continuum. Eternity was not for them a destination out in the great beyond. The Celts believed we live eternity in the here and now. They looked upon earth as an *anam cara*, a soul friend. The earth's core is its most ancient part. It holds both the secrets of creation and echoes of eternity.

Most days I wake in a hurry to get on to the "important" business of the day ahead. Doing so, I undoubtedly miss a good deal of what is truly important.

Mid-winter mornings are especially dark and quiet. They remind us to slow down, listen, look and look again. On those days when I am attentive, I feel as though I can hear murmurs of the secrets that earth holds in its breast. By pausing occasionally, instead of rushing on to the next place or the next task, I find I still accomplish what I need to do, and much more.

GOD, THE EXISTING

I rake leaves in wind
Neighbor calls, "They'll just blow back"
This is my zazen

JV

Zazen is the Buddhist practice that urges us to pay attention to the task at hand. For example, in autumn, it's tempting to look upon leave-raking as just another nuisance that eats up my precious free time. But I can just as well consider this work an opening to meditation.

As I cleared the lawn on a particularly windy day, my neighbor called to me with what I'm sure she considered some sensible advice. Why on earth would I try to rake leaves in such wind? She could not know that forming the leaves into neat piles was not my main purpose. Raking offered a break from the mental activity of my regular work, writing. It gave me time to slow down and focus on one simple task. I can bring this kind of mindfulness to chores I really don't like doing, like ironing or washing the dishes.

A friend of mine, the late spiritual writer Brother Wayne Teasdale, hated flying. Yet he jetted all over the world teaching and lecturing. I asked him how he managed it. He said he turned every flight into a continuous meditation. That kind of mindfulness transforms any task — whether welcome or not — into zazen. To quote the late Benedictine writer Imogene Baker, it is form of contemplation to simply "be where you are, and do what you're doing."

GOD, THE PEACEFUL ONE

Lamplit cubicles
High rise bee combs glow in night
Abuzz with stories

J V

For years I worked at home in a high rise overlooking one of the busiest streets in Chicago. Perched on the fifteenth floor, I could hear the hiss of air brakes on public buses, the beat of a hip hop song pounding out of a car radio or stray bits of conversation emanating from other apartments. In summer, jackhammers blasted and cement mixers roared in the business of street repairs. It was impossible to find even a few moments of continuous silence. Even in the college town of Normal, Illinois, where I now live, the whine of lawn mowers drowns out any semblance of quiet on weekend mornings. In autumn, it's the buzz of leaf blowers.

In our culture, silence is an endangered species. In 1968, it took fifteen hours of recording time to obtain a single uninterrupted hour of nature sounds. Today, it takes two thousand hours of recording time to get one hour of sound without a car engine starting or a jet roaring overhead. And yet, silence is essential for our inner life, just as water and protein are for a healthy body. When a day offers some respite for silence, it is pure gift. More times than not, I have to give that gift to myself. It may mean shutting the windows for a while each day to block out the noise, or finding the quietest place I can within the hubbub of the city. It may be a church pew or a park bench or a rooftop.

From eight o'clock in the evening until eight in the morning, Trappist monks observe what they call The Grand Silence. Trappists long ago recognized that silence is the deepest form of prayer. Can I carve out my own Grand Silence, starting, say, with ten minutes each day? Can I make of that silence one continuous prayer?

GOD, THE RESTORER

Home for wounded souls:
could purgatory exist
anywhere but earth?

J V

In the Christian tradition, November is a time for remembering the dead. In the northern hemisphere, flowers crumble, leaves wither. Morning frosts prepare us for the barrenness of winter when, as Thomas Merton writes, "the plant says nothing." All Soul's Day is a time to pray for "the poor souls in Purgatory," the spiritual terrain believed to exist between heaven and hell.

Some theologians believe there isn't a separate sphere where souls are sent to be "purified" before they can enter paradise. Life on earth, they say, is all we need of purgatory. Perhaps earth is equal parts *inferno*, *purgatorio* and *paradiso* all wrapped into one. The ancient Celts believed the dead are ever present, only we, in our limited consciousness, can't see them. But occasionally we can intuit their presence in what the Celts called the "thin places."

I like to think of this life as a bridge between the place we arrived from at birth and the place to which we are going. In his poem, "The Hammock," the poet Li-Young Lee refers to this life an "interlude between two great rests." When I remember those who have passed on, I think of them not in some intermediate way station called Purgatory, but right here next to me, close enough to reach out and touch.

GOD, THE AFFIRMING

A man far off dies
His death is like a pin dropping
Yet soundlessly felt

JV

My friend Brother Paul Quenon of the Abbey of Gethsemani sent out a message recently informing friends that one of his fellow monks had passed away. I did not know Brother Rene Richie well. I met him only once. He was leading some formal prayers in the small chapel across from the abbey's main church. What struck me was that whenever he stopped to add a personal prayer, it was not a prayer of petition: *Please God help me with* …. His were prayers of thanksgiving … for the gift of existence … for the mercy of God … for the strength to work another day. Brother Rene was about to spend two weeks at the University of Kentucky Hospital in Louisville undergoing treatment for throat cancer. He died a few weeks later.

A friend of mine makes a point of praying daily for "all the people who will die today and especially those who will die alone." The Benedictine sisters of Mount St. Scholastica in Atchison, Kansas pray each week for "the next member of our community who will enter eternity." It is a beautiful prayer ministry. I'd like to think someone will be praying like that for me when my time comes.

Whenever someone passes from this life, we lose a piece of what the novelist Paulo Coehlo calls "the soul of the world," though that person's death may be as soundless to us as a pin dropping. Today, I pause to honor those souls that will pass from this world. I bless the new souls waiting to be born.

GOD, THE DISTRESSER

Tree trunk without bark
some unknown illness suffered:
my own wounded skin

JV

For many years I attended the 5:30 p.m. daily Mass at my neighborhood parish. The same young man usually read the first reading and the responsorial psalm. His neck was deeply scarred, as if it had been badly burned. It must have taken courage for him to stand up in public and display those physical scars.

Throughout my life, I've expended a great deal of energy trying to hide the kind of scars that aren't visible. And yet, isn't everyone in some way wounded? The apostle Paul wrote of suffering a "sting to the flesh" that he sometimes found unbearable. Perhaps it wasn't even a physical wound, but some kind of inner pain. All we know is the sting never left him. What changed was his attitude about it. He came to accept it as part of who he was. "When I am weak," he concluded, "then I am strong."

I once covered a story for PBS-TV about a spiritual retreat for survivors of clergy abuse. "I know why you are all here," the retreat leader said on the first night. "You're here because you feel that something inside you is broken, and you want someone or something to fix it. I'm here to tell you, there's nothing to be fixed, because there's nothing broken." Over the course of several days, the counselor helped these survivors see that the experience of abuse they endured was broken, but they were not. I can chose to turn away from my injured places — my wounded ego, character flaws, physical imperfections and deep-seated hurts. Or I can look upon them as thresholds for discovering the true self. Like Paul, like those survivors of abuse, I can transform this brokenness. When I am weak, I am strong.

GOD, THE DEFENDER AND SHIELDER

Earth mover downs five oaks
As if fired upon, they fall
Crack! Heave a last groan

JV

One of the most memorable people I have interviewed as a journalist is the late Nobel Peace Prize winner Wangari Maathai. Dr. Maathai's Green Belt Movement put thousands of African women to work planting trees. Because of her efforts, more than a billion trees have been planted worldwide. Trees not only replace the oxygen we breathe. Their roots help hold top soil and ground water in place, essentials for farming. Dr. Maathai witnessed the destruction of thousands of trees in her native Kenya. From her days as a biology student at Mount St. Scholastica College in Kansas, she began to connect deforestation with the growing water crisis in Africa. Where there is scarcity of resources, there is conflict, she would say. She spent the rest of her life trying to convince world leaders that care of the environment is also a path to peace.

When my husband and I purchased some farmland in central Illinois, we decided to dig a lake on the property to attract and sustain wildlife. The only drawback was that we had to uproot several dozen trees in the process. Every time our farmer friend mowed down one of the trees with his earth mover, I felt as though I was witnessing a death by firing squad. Like a wounded soldier, each tree fell with a piercing groan I will never forget. There was no doubt that a living thing had collapsed.

When the Abbey of Gethsemani had to cut down one of its oldest oaks, the monks marked the occasion with a smudging ceremony, a ritual borrowed from Native Americans. They burned sage blessed by a medicine man and let the smoke pour over the spot where the tree had stood. Then they planted a new tree. My husband and I have replaced some of the trees we removed, but surely not enough. Dr. Maathai often told audiences that it takes two new trees to restore the oxygen a single person removes from the atmosphere in an average lifetime. She would tell audiences in her booming melodic voice, "Whenever you see a tree, you thank that tree for helping to keep you alive!" Wangari Maathai died in the fall of 2011 at the age of 71. Her spirit continues to reach the far corners of the world in each new tree that is planted.

GOD, THE DETERMINER

World Series over
Into winners and losers
life divides again

JV

Baseball just may be the most spiritual of sports. It is played in the open air (unless, of course, you attend a home game of the Minnesota Twins or Houston Astros and have to sit in a covered arena. Boring!). Like a good worship service, baseball unites strangers within the same space for a common purpose. It isn't ruled by a clock, like football or basketball, but proceeds for however many innings it takes to break a tie score. Conceivably, a tie game could continue on into perpetuity. And like most spiritual seekers, baseball's runners are always trying to get home. While I love the World Series, I can never bear to watch the final out. Inevitably, the camera pans from the jubilant winners on the field to the losing team's players as they lumber out of their dugout, looking as though their mascot had just been shot. Up until that point, both teams could be called "winners."

When I was in college, all I could think about was getting a job at a big newspaper. I soon got my wish. *The Washington Post*, one of the best newspapers in the country, wanted to hire me as soon as I graduated. I later moved on to an even larger paper, *The Wall Street Journal*. Reporters competed daily to place their stories on that prime piece of real estate, the front page. It never occurred to me that just getting a story published between the front section and the stock quotes was a win too.

Papua New Guinea, a small Pacific island, may not seem like a trendsetter. But we might take a cue from the islanders there. They celebrate both the winning and losing team in equal measure. In his poem, "Steps," Frank O'Hara includes a few lines about the 1961 Pittsburgh Pirates' surprise win in the World Series. Like the people of Papua New Guinea, O'Hara had the right idea. "We're all winning," he wrote in his poem. "We're alive."

GOD, THE ALL-SEEING

A solo cricket
plays his one-stringed violin—
stroke, pause, stroke, pause, pause

PQ

Late in autumn, when temperatures dip, there is something pathetic, yet brave, about a particular sound rising up out of the ground. Like an old musician playing a dated repertoire, the cricket continues on with its feeble song because that is the only song it knows. The cricket's low strokes continue even when no one is listening, not even other crickets, who perhaps are already asleep. Even with the passion gone, something rather sweet rises with the cricket's song, something slow and lingering

What will remain of my prayer when old age comes on? Sometimes at our abbey, monks would ask their novice director, our late Father Louis (Thomas Merton), why some of the more senior monks did not seem to have a deep spiritual life. He would explain that they certainly did have one, but that very personal part of their lives was now more inward and hidden.

What of my effort will remain? Will it be a slowing down, something long drawn out, like the cricket's tune? Or does prayer resign itself to silence and rest when the better part of the work is done? Will it even matter in the endless summer of eternity, which makes and remakes seasons for us all — and the cricket?

GOD, THE INCOMPARABLE

Grandmother's house-odors:
linoleum, iron, dry lace,
cooking gas, roast beef

PQ

Memory, with its frail, winding threads of scents, can conjure up an entire household. A scent may be the first or the last, the strongest or the least thing we notice when entering a house. Some scents are no longer detected in modern homes. My mother and her mother took pride in hand-washing their lace curtains with a sweet-smelling soap. They stretched them on a pin frame to dry and then hung them on a curtain rod — a job I eventually inherited. Does anyone hand-wash curtains anymore? Nowadays, everything is sprayed with Febreze.

The hermitage where Thomas Merton lived in the last years of his life offers its own distinctive mood of odors: wood smoke residue from the fireplace and walls; the raw, concrete smell of bare unpainted cinder block and the mountain-air scent of its redwood furnishings. A unique blend.

Our monastery, before its renovation, smelled of plaster, must, aged wood, and, during humid seasons, mold on whitewash. As a novice, I got the job of wiping mold off the damp walls and repainting them. The brick and terrazzo surface of our renovated abbey is mostly odorless. It lacks that thin thread of scent that tugs at awareness in the soul. Memory goes without.

GOD, THE HUMBLER

I've nothing to do
So I'll get down to nothing
Expeditiously

PQ

GOD, THE BRINGER OF DEATH

Bier returned empty
from graveside, surface rumpled,
eased by subtraction

PQ

Every Trappist monk is buried directly in the ground without a coffin. A reusable homemade bier transports the body to the abbey church and later to the grave site. Then the bier is returned to storage to await the next burial.

Brother Thaddeus was my age and entered the monastery the same year as I did. Later in life, he was overweight, suffered from diabetes, and endured many other health problems. He bore his infirmities with humor. He would frequently lose his balance and fall. I asked him if he knew what caused this. "I must have dropsy," he said. His death was so sudden that the shock of it unsettled us all. But he had suffered so much during life we were relieved that his departure had not been a protracted one.

After decades of living in community with an individual, one begins to rely on the familiar face, the solid body to be there. Even the particular disabilities of that body are part of the daily routine one lives with, be it with empathy or even annoyance. Then one day what seemed a firm stepping stone suddenly becomes a gap to jump over, a pothole underfoot, where before the street had been smooth and solid.

GOD, THE EXALTER

Monks walk past foot light
Cast huge shadows on church wall
— fugitive giants.

PQ

At night the monastery's long hallways and high-ceiled church are darkened. There is only enough light to help us navigate from one end to the other. Twice a week we say Vigils at three in the morning in the abbey church with just one lamp lit at the lectern. Various readers take turns reciting the Psalms and Scripture, while the rest of the community listens quietly in the dark. Moonlight sometimes softens the rough walls and peers through blackened windows.

It is during the Night Office especially that we read about danger, treacherous enemies and the searing hostilities that David, the warrior King, experienced. The Book of Revelation with its frightening images never sounds more disconcerting than when the mind is still close to dream time after a long night's sleep.

This is the hour of imagination at free-play, and the hour to take refuge under the shadow of God's wing. Outdoors, the November skies may brood dark and low, or the summer sky may open to disclose the Great Bear, the Lion or Scorpio posed to sting. Monks love the dark. It is a country of our own. The looming shadows are not entirely pretend ones, because we know in the mind there is much worse to deal with — shadows of our own making. It is a good practice to acclimatize ourselves to interior reality by being immersed in the outer darkness. But still, in the midst of it, there are distant points of light and familiar lines of God's word to guide us along the way. They seem more prized than ever in the darkness.

GOD, THE MAGNIFICENT

Signs of blight showing —
magnificent sycamore —
Ah, the world's changing!

PQ

The Abbey of Gethsemani is home to what just may be the largest sycamore tree in all of Kentucky. Anyone who draws near it is awed by its massive, other-worldly white trunk. Visitors who come here regularly for retreats sometimes ask for a room with a view of this tree. It is a living landmark. Its size and longevity define the location where it sits, so when such a remarkable landmark goes, it seems the world around it changes too.

How many monks have I known, larger than life, who have passed? Each one by his presence redefined the profile of the monastery where I live. As a result, I have lived in many monasteries over the years, though I have never left this place.

It is time's gift to all of us that everything changes and yet stays the same.

GOD, THE ALMIGHTY

Memory of our bull —
How he let me rub his eyes
Between us a sweet trust

PQ

Years ago the monastery where I live had a dairy herd that included the prize-winning bulls, Astronaut and Orbiter. Both seemed to weigh a ton. Orbiter was penned behind a fence made of three-inch thick pipes. I once stood safely on the other side and tried to befriend him.

To tease a penned bull was out of the question for me. I knew full well that at another monastery one of the brothers had made that mistake. He sat on the fence and plied his belt to agitate the bull. The bull not only knocked this brother to the ground, but then crushed his hip with its head.

I hadn't the nerve to sit on the fence, but from the safe side I wanted to see if Orbiter would let me pet him. It took time. First I let his curiosity grow until he approached on his own. He wanted to know my scent. So I exhaled my breath, lent my hand and my skin to smell. He touched with his nose, the first touch; then I touched his nose and gradually moved to furry areas. The eyes are the most vulnerable area, the most sensitive, and once confidence was established, I rubbed the area around his eyes. I thought he might enjoy that. A bull's eyes are frequently tortured by flies which he cannot rub away on his own. My touch was a new sensation for the bull. I went away with a new assurance that love can be found everywhere.

GOD, THE MOST HIGH

Boy with camera
shoots at the moon, wants moon tucked
snug in his pocket.

PQ

As an avid photographer, I have never understood why someone would want a close-up shot of the moon. The moon always looks the same. One can get splendid close-ups of any phase of it from NASA's website. So there must be something gratifying about having taken the picture personally, poor as the quality may be. It might arise from some instinct to possess the unreachable. A picture of the moon is pretty tawdry compared to the actual thing, yet I suppose you can derive a secret satisfaction in hiding it away on your person. Usually this is a beginner's instinct, or perhaps fetishism, soon cured by taking a number of disappointing images.

I once heard a young bride say her husband would buy her the moon if she asked him. I hope she never asked — it would break the love-spell.

I believe the only way to relate to the transcendent is to let it remain transcendent — which it will in any case. The heart must remain free of the poison of idolatry, the first and chief temptation, given prominence of place in the Ten Commandments as the first sin forbidden. Yet we continue to claim to possess the transcendent. We photograph the moon, as it were, and tuck it in close by, feeling satisfied we have captured what we can never own.

GOD, THE COMFORTER

After long rainfall
Leftover music dribbles
Dancing on puddles

PQ

I sometimes sit under an overhanging roof meditating outdoors in the rain. It is tempting to overlook or ignore the undramatic mood of slow rain, especially compared to the rash wildness of storms. Yet a soft rain is quietly agreeable. It is also compatible with recollection — a gathering of the mind into a still inner space. A gentle rain evokes intimacy. It is something not so much to watch, as to wait out and wait with. It rarely provokes a comment to the neighbor; it simply remains one's own.

Prayer too is something we don't ordinarily talk about, and all the better for that reason. Like quiet rain, prayer carries a contentment that swells imperceptibly in privacy.

As Emily Dickinson said in her angular way: "In many and reportless places we feel a joy."

GOD, THE OWNER OF ALL SOVEREIGNTY

With big, white flashlight
moon is walking its night-rounds
asking: who are you?

PQ

Our monastery is so large and isolated and free of city light that a pure kind of darkness often washes over it. Moonlight can surprise us in the middle of the night, a bold intruder.

Once I dreamed a watchman had shone a light on my bed. I urged myself awake for this rude stranger and found it was the moon.

Perhaps the dream contained more truth than I supposed: the full moon is a kind of watchman who has looked over this place every month since forever. I am the one who is the intruder — a passing sojourner. In the larger scheme of things, I must content myself at being a short-term transient in an extremely ancient moonlife.

GOD THE UTTERLY JUST

At a cruel moment
Jesus stooped, scrawled in dust
Best haiku ever—

PQ

In a famous Scripture story, society's elders bring to Jesus a woman caught in adultery. They ready themselves for judgment and a stoning. But Jesus simply stoops down and writes with his finger something in the dusty soil. To this day, no one knows exactly what Jesus wrote. It was enough, apparently, to send the crowd slinking away.

Silence — not making a reply — is Jesus' way of replying. His judgment is to make no judgment. The gesture speaks for itself. He removes himself from the heat of the moment and lowers himself to touch the earth, the mother and equalizer of us all.

Perhaps Jesus inscribed a single word. In a sense, each of us is our own unique word, embedded in dust. I sometimes imagine that Jesus wrote a short poem, perhaps even haiku-like, that struck at the heart of our human propensity for condemnation and judgment. In the making of art, beauty becomes an answer to life's folly and ugliness. It brings something transcendent to bear on that which is the opposite. Art offers a pathway to freedom and detachment, an intimation that life can be other. Art will not save the world, but it suggests that the world can be saved. Art is the deep breath Jesus took to rupture the connection between accusation and condemnation, to open up a wider vision of the world—one shaped by forgiveness and a divine judgment utterly new to our understanding.

GOD, THE PRAISEWORTHY

Pensive comes autumn
Color drains from summer cheeks
Breeze on flesh chilling

MB

I once witnessed former U.S. Poet Laureate W. S. Merwin hold an audience spellbound for more than two hours as he read his poetry. In between poems, there was the usual rustle of chairs, clearing of throats, but no talking. Behind his magnificent words lay a curtain of silence.

When Merwin finished reading, there was a moment when no one moved. Then the very literary chap next to me whispered in my ear, "He seemed a bit wistful tonight." Great poets often grow more contemplative as they age, seeking out imagery that draws on memory.

Autumn is such a season: pensive, but still jubilant; a time of fullness, memory and recollection. The browning leaves themselves and the fainter slant of the sun remind us that time is fleeting. From the first to the last leaf that falls, we experience a crisper, cooler time. Time to ready again for the inexorable winter.

GOD, THE KNOWER

Same time, place last year
Old man sealed a sacred pact
He left before spring

MB

It is October again. The leaves deepen to gold and crimson, and I find myself once more at the Abbey of Gethsemani. In the sixteen years I have been coming to this monastery, Father Matthew Kelty, a priest "according to the order of Melchizedek" and Trappist monk for more than half a century, has graced each of my visits.

Last year at this time, he placed around my neck a small, silver "miracle medal" with the face of Jesus' mother on it. I have never removed it. Last October, sitting under the evergreens in front of Gethsemani, we spoke of many things, as always. I finally felt bold enough to tell him that he is the Friend for whom I have yearned all of my life. He told me he would always be with me.

And so it is as the leaves turn color and a brisk October wind blows between the white crosses of the abbey cemetery.

GOD, THE ONE

Two blue chairs sitting
One contemplates brass Buddha
Other simply sits

MB

GOD, THE PROPITIOUS

Sipping cup of tea
Planets are born, worlds emerge
Drink to the last drop

MB

If nectar is the drink of gods, tea is certainly the drink of spiritual masters. One Zen master is said to have turned away would-be acolytes with the admonition, "Better to have a cup of tea!" Another would say to those who came to him seeking marvels, mysteries and epiphanies, "What is the whole experience? Go back and have some tea." And the eighteenth century Japanese poet, Baisao, known as "The Old Tea Seller," wrote:

> *Sake fuels the vital spirits, works like courage,*
> *Tea works benevolently, purifying the soul.*
> *Courageous feats that put the world in your debt*
> *Couldn't match the benefits benevolence brings.*

In this soul-stifling age of instant gratification, I honor the slow, small movements of brewing tea. All the epiphanies I can handle come to me as I sit quietly on my front porch, savoring each fresh cup.

GOD, THE CREATOR

Taverna of song
In Leonard Cohen's warm chair
Spirits at sundown

MB

Leonard Cohen is a poet, singer and songwriter of surpassing talent. He is equally a man of the spirit, a sincere and persistent seeker who lived for ten years on Mount Baldy in California as a practicing Zen monk. He's the real deal, as those who know him would say. Eventually his passion for life, poetry and song propelled him back to the stage. His gravelly baritone and poetic lyrics cast a spell on audiences around the world.

In the days he lived as a monk, Cohen occasionally came down the mountain to visit one of my local hangouts, a venerable Greek taverna in the heart of Claremont, California. He had a favorite chair out front where he would sip ouzo and watch the sunset. He told my friend Jim, the taverna owner, that he needed a spot of ouzo now and then because, "Being a monk is damn hard!"

As I sat in his old chair one night, watching the sun go down, a patron mistook me for Cohen. A compliment indeed. For a moment, I thought I heard him harmonizing with the troubadours on the street. "Just payin' my rent everyday, in the tower of song." A worthy vocation.

GOD, THE KING

Going and coming
Brittle wind whips my old shirt
Such an ideal home

MB

GOD, THE INDEPENDENT

Already empty
Still breathing through clear windows
House of no abode

MB

Remembrance of things past, taught novelist Marcel Proust, marks the heart of awareness. Maybe so. A venerable house to the north of ours stands empty. It breathes deeply as if in meditation, perhaps remembering something of the long past.

Locals gossiped that the neighbors who had lived there suddenly uprooted and moved to the beach. I noticed they were gone one morning when I woke up to the strangest of sensations: pure quiet. I looked out the window and saw the old place was empty. Thus it remains: at rest, at peace, in stillness, like a leafless tree in autumn — a transformed, but no less welcome presence in our community.

This house of no abode reminds me to cultivate an inner stillness of pure quiet.

GOD, THE LAST

Gray mist between trees:
Portal we pass through en route
To new adventures

JV

AUTHOR BIOGRAPHIES

Judith Valente is an on air correspondent for the national PBS-TV news show, *Religion & Ethics NewsWeekly*. Her reports have also appeared on National Public Radio and *The NewsHour* on PBS. She is the author of the poetry collections *Inventing An Alphabet*, selected by Mary Oliver for the 2005 Aldrich Poetry Prize, and *Discovering Moons* (Virtual Artists Collective, Chicago, 2009). She is co-editor with Charles Reynard of *Twenty Poems to Nourish Your Soul* (Loyola Press, Chicago, 2005), an anthology of poems and reflections on finding the sacred in the ordinary. The anthology won an Eric Hoffer Book Award citation. She worked previously as a staff writer for *The Washington Post* and *The Wall Street Journal*. She is the author of the non-fiction book, *Atchison Blue: A Search for Silence, a Spiritual Home and a Living Faith* (Sorin Books, 2013), which chronicles her experiences as a regular visitor to Mount St. Scholastica Monastery in Atchison, Kansas. She is married to Illinois Circuit Court Judge Charles Reynard, also a poet. The couple has led numerous spirituality retreats across the country. She and her husband live in Chicago and Normal, Illinois, and operate an alfalfa farm in Woodford County, Illinois.

Brother Paul Quenon has been a monk of the Abbey of Gethsemani since 1958. He has published four books of poetry, most recently *Afternoons with Emily* (Windsor, Ont., Black Moss Press, 2011) and *Monkswear* (Louisville, Fons Vitae, 2008); and a recent anthology of poetry and writings about monasticism *Monkscript Two: Surprising Saints* (Louisville, Fons Vitae, 2012). For seven years, he has used Haiku as an organic part of his daily meditation, seated not far outside the church, overlooking the fields, slopes and hills of Kentucky where monks have lived over 160 years.

Michael Bever is a freelance writer, poet, and editor. He has been a radio personality, a university dean and a pastor. He has contributed to Religion Dispatches, Odyssey Networks, and *Harper's Weekly*. He was co-editor with Paul Quenon of the poetry anthology, *Monkscript Two: Surprising Saints* (Fons Vitae). His film and video work includes his documentary, *This Lone Brightness*, featuring his friend Father Matthew Kelty, OCSO, and work with an Emmy nominated PBS documentary (*The Presidency, the Press, and the People*, 1990). He holds a doctorate from the Claremont School of Theology and has been influenced by Zen and catholic traditions as presented in the life and work of Thomas Merton. He lives in Claremont, California, with his wife Rena, an administrator at Claremont McKenna College. In addition to various literary involvements, he serves as Associate Director of the Robert and Frances Flaherty Film Study Center at Claremont.

ACKNOWLEDGMENTS

Grateful acknowledgment is extended to Gregory Pierce, president of ACTA Publications, for his guidance, enthusiasm for this project and his masterful editing, and to Charles G. Reynard, for being a critical first reader of the manuscript.

SUGGESTIONS FOR FURTHER READING

Haiku Mind: 108 Poems to Cultivate Awareness and Open Your Heart. Patricia Donegan. Shambala. 2008

Given. Wendell Berry. Shoemaker Hoard/Avalon Publishing. 2005.

A Short History of Nearly Everything. Bill Bryson. Broadway Books. 2003.

The Intimate Merton: His Life from His Journals. HarperOne. 1999.

Anam Cara: A Book of Celtic Wisdom. John O'Donohue. HarperCollins. 1998.

Eternal Echoes: Celtic Reflections on Our Yearning to Belong. HarperCollins. 1999.

Seven Sacred Pauses: Living Mindfully Through the Hours of the Day. Macrina Wiederkehr. Sorin Books. 2008.

Man's Search for Meaning. Viktor E. Frankl. Beacon Press. 1959.

Twenty Poems to Nourish Your Soul. Edited by Judith Valente and Charles Reynard. Loyola Press. 2005.

Monkscript. Edited by Paul Quenon. Fons Vitae. 2002.

Afternoons with Emily. Paul Quenon. Black Moss Press. 2011.

My Song is of Mercy: Writings of Matthew Kelty, Monk of Gethsemani. Edited by Michael Downey. Sheed & Ward. 1994.